JFK & Jackie

Unseen Archives

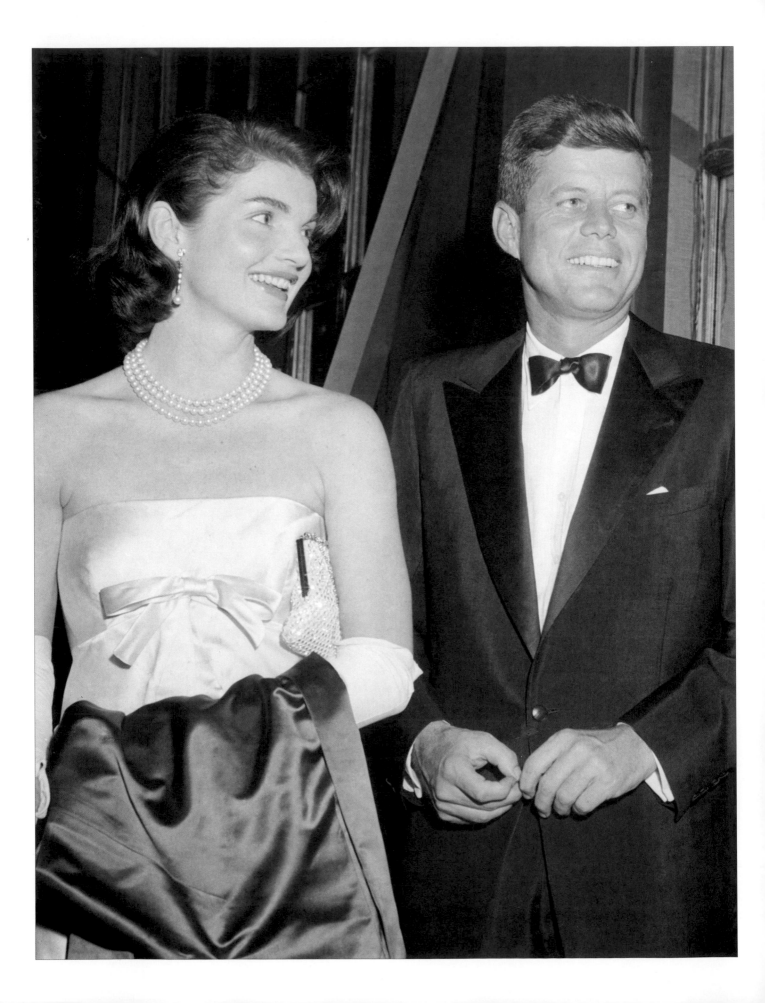

JFK & Jackie

Unseen Archives

TIM HILL

This is a Parragon Publishing Book
This edition published in 2005

Parragon Publishing
Queen Street House
4 Queen Street
Bath
BA1 1HE, UK

Text © Parragon
For details of photographs see pages 382-383

Produced by Atlantic Publishing
Designed by John Dunne

ISBN 1-40546-738-X

Printed in China

Contents

Introduction

John F. Kennedy was the voice of a generation. The youngest man ever to be elected to the White House, he transcended politics, inspiring people the world over with his ideals, vision and boundless energy to reach "new frontiers". Jacqueline Kennedy was intelligent, cultured and beautiful. The President and First Lady were a golden couple, enjoying the kind of celebrity normally reserved for Hollywood stars.

These bald facts obscure as much as they reveal. JFK was a reluctant politician, lacking both conviction and application as a young Congressman. Marriage to Jackie was at least in part politically motivated, and didn't curb his serial womanizing. He grew in stature while in office, and may have gone on to achieve true greatness. After the events in Dallas on 22 November 1963, the world remembered JFK, not so much for his achievements, but for what he represented and what might have been.

JFK & Jackie: Unseen Archives charts the rise to power of a political giant. It also recounts the key moments in a marriage which survived betrayal and tragedy. The detailed commentary, together with more than 400 photographs, gives a fascinating insight into the public and private faces of JFK and Jackie, disentangling myth from reality.

When John F. Kennedy narrowly beat Richard Nixon in the presidential election of November 1960, it was the realization of a dream. The man who had harbored that dream longest was not Jack, but his father. Joseph Kennedy instilled in all his children a fierce competitiveness. They were expected to aim high, and finishing second simply wasn't good enough. Politically, there was no greater goal than the White House itself. That would undoubtedly have been the target for Joseph Kennedy Jr, Jack's elder brother and the golden boy of the family. When he was killed in action during World War Two, the hopes and expectations of the family turned to the second-born, John F. Kennedy.

His early political career was undistinguished. After doing what the Kennedys were good at - winning - he found the daily grind of public life largely unappealing. Sports and socializing were more to his liking, with womanizing high on his list of recreational activities. He was no ideologue, and even made a virtue out of his lack of conviction. But he had good looks, charisma, charm and wit, which his political opponents would underestimate to their cost.

Jack Kennedy was made for the televisual age. The image was of robust vitality. Here was a man with the dynamism and energy to galvanize the country after the steady but uninspiring Eisenhower years. It mattered little that, far from being vigorous and athletic, Kennedy was dogged by ill health. As his father had taught him, it wasn't what you were that counted, but what people thought you were.

Perception and reality were at variance in other ways too. JFK was feted as a war hero, despite the mystery surrounding the loss of his vessel and the deaths of two crewmen; he came from one of the richest families in the country, yet was notoriously parsimonious; he was represented as an idealist, but was instinctively pragmatic; he liked to associate himself with intellectuals and artists, yet was not above secret meetings with mobsters; the rhetoric of his speeches was unforgettable, but in private he was much given to oaths and expletives.

The gap between image and reality became a yawning chasm when it came to marriage. Almost inevitably, Joe Kennedy had a hand in what was seen as a fairytale union. Jacqueline Bouvier had the elegance, glamor and class befitting the role of the young candidate's wife. For her part, Jackie was dazzled by the thought that one of the most eligible bachelors in the land would pay attention to her. A difficult relationship with her mother had left her with low self-esteem, though both knew the importance of making a good match. The

courtship was less romantic, and Jackie was soon disabused of the notion that a piece of paper would signal an end to her husband's bachelor lifestyle.

JFK took the oath of office on 20 January 1961. It was the beginning of a decade which would become synonymous with hope and optimism. Kennedy captured the spirit of the age, and his appeal stretched far beyond the political arena and far beyond America's shores.

The fruits of JFK's 1000 days in office were not overly spectacular. The Peace Corps and Alliance For Progress were worthy initiatives. He gave both vocal and financial support to the space race, accurately predicting that America would put a man on the moon before the decade was out. The nuclear test ban treaty, signed in October 1963, stands as one of his greatest achievements. On the downside, the Bay of Pigs invasion of Cuba in 1961 ended in a humiliating defeat. And when the USA and the Soviet Union brought the world to the brink of nuclear conflagration in 1962, Kennedy had luck on his side as well as judgment. On the issue of civil rights he vacillated for a long time, and the promised legislation would only be enacted after his death.

By the fall of 1963, JFK was maturing into an outstanding statesman. A new moral dimension informed his decision-making, and he was determined to do what was right, even if it carried political risks. The first term, with its narrow mandate, had laid the foundations; the second would see great strides on both the domestic and international fronts. The events of 22 November 1963 changed all that. The crusading idealist had become a martyr to his cause. Almost immediately he was transformed into an untouchable hero. His virtues and achievements became the stuff of legend, his vices and failures were studiously overlooked. For a time, to challenge this orthodoxy was tantamount to heresy. Jackie won universal admiration for the dignity with which she bore her loss. She put aside her disdain for politics and the pain of infidelity to ensure that her husband's memory was preserved for posterity.

JFK had wanted to usher in a golden age of poetry and power. His reputation would become tarnished with the passage of time, yet he carried with him the hopes of a generation and remains a giant on the political landscape of the twentieth century.

Acknowledgements

This book would not have been possible without the help of
Jonathan Hamston, Matt Smithson, Giovanni D'Angelico,
Maria Lopez-Duran, Zohir Naciri and Scott Kirkham.
Thanks also to
Richard Betts, Laura and Jennifer Hill and
Nicola and Mollie Richardson.

JFK & Jackie

Unseen Archives

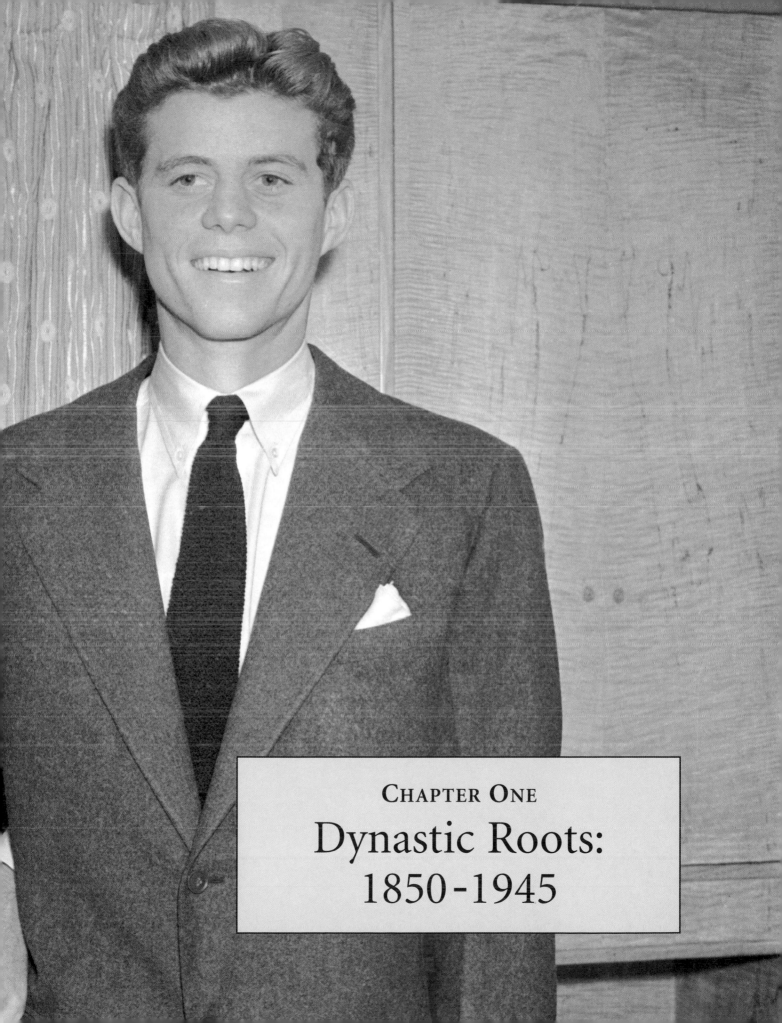

CHAPTER ONE

Dynastic Roots:
1850-1945

John Fitzgerald Kennedy was born on 29 May 1917, the second son to Joseph and Rose Kennedy. The path to the White House may not have been clearly mapped out for the new arrival. However, many of the elements which marked Jack out for high office were already in place. Politics was in the blood, on both his father's and mother's side; drive, ambition and the will to succeed, at almost any cost, was imbued in him from an early age, and the family was wealthy and well connected. Of course, all of these factors were equally applicable to Jack's elder brother, Joe Jr But when Joe was killed in action during World War Two, it was on the second son's shoulders that the hopes and expectations of the family primarily rested.

Many critical decisions propelled JFK to the White House, with serendipity playing its part. The first of these occurred sixty-nine years before Jack was born, when Patrick Kennedy, his great-grandfather, decided to join the teeming exodus from Ireland in the wake of the Potato Famine. Twenty-six-year-old Patrick was better placed than most to withstand the hardships. His family grew barley and raised cattle in County Wexford, one of the areas least affected by the blight. But he wanted to broaden his horizons and make his fortune, and so he chose to take his chance along with hordes of his countrymen

in the famous "coffin ships" bound for the USA. Many who paid the $12 fare for the grueling six-week journey perished on the way. Patrick was one of the fortunate ones; Bridget Murphy was another. The two struck up a relationship during the crossing, and they would marry in September of the following year.

Patrick and Bridget disembarked in Boston, and, like many of their fellow emigrants, they settled there. This was primarily an economic decision, for few had the resources to go further afield.

The Kennedys soon found that this was no land of milk and honey. Living conditions were harsh and all those of Irish extraction were subjected to prejudice and hostility from the indigenous population. By the 1850s, when employers and landlords posted advertisements, the acronym "NINA" was a common sight. No Irish Need Apply. The establishment was Anglo-Saxon and Protestant. Irish Catholics were looked upon with suspicion and contempt. The Boston where Patrick and Bridget began married life was full of Irish ghettoes, as both sides eschewed assimilation. Like many others, they were in danger of simply exchanging rural poverty in Ireland for urban poverty in America, and being relegated to underclass status into the bargain.

Patrick found work as a cooper, while Bridget gave birth to four children in quick succession. The youngest, Patrick Joseph, was born on 14 January 1858. Patrick didn't live to see his son's first birthday, succumbing to cholera two months short of that anniversary. He would be the last of the Kennedy line to die in poverty and obscurity.

The young Patrick, known as PJ, was ambitious

Opposite: Patrick Joseph Kennedy, the paternal grandfather of John F. Kennedy. PJ embodied two of the main Kennedy traits: he was both a natural entrepreneur and a political animal. By the mid 1880s, he was running a thriving liquor business and rising through the ranks of the Democratic Party in East Boston.

and hard-working. Some of his early endeavors in his teenage years were in the shipyards, where he worked as a stevedore. This supplemented the family income, his mother having turned to shop work and hairdressing after Patrick's death. When he was in his early twenties, PJ bought a run-down saloon, the first step on the way to a successful business career. He eventually owned a chain of bars, and expanded his empire by moving into the wholesale side of the liquor business too.

PJ's talents also found a natural home in the political arena. The expatriate Irish community formed bar-room associations which soon began to dominate local Democratic Party structures. This was done partly by sheer weight of numbers and partly by some underhand vote-rigging. In 1886 PJ Kennedy began the first of five consecutive terms in the Massachusetts House of Representatives, and in 1892 he was admitted to the state senate. He quickly added political skills to business acumen. A consummate pragmatist, PJ knew how power and influence were wielded. Perhaps more importantly, he knew what it took to win, something which would become a Kennedy trait.

In 1887 PJ married Mary Augusta Hickey, the daughter of a prosperous businessman. His mother died the following year, having lived just long enough to see the birth of the couple's first child. Joseph, born on 6 September 1888, was to be the father of the thirty-fifth president of the United States.

By the turn of the century, PJ Kennedy was one of the pre-eminent politicians in Boston. Another was John Francis Fitzgerald, himself a second generation Irish immigrant. A silky-tongued charmer and a larger-than-life character, he became known as "Honey Fitz". He too was elected to the state senate in 1892, where he served alongside PJ. The two men had little time for each other. Honey Fitz went on to serve in Congress, and in 1905 he became Boston's first mayor to be born of Irish parents.

The friction between PJ Kennedy and Honey Fitz was eventually tempered when the two families were joined in marriage. PJ's son, Joseph, married Honey Fitz's eldest daughter, Rose, who was the apple of his eye. Joseph and Rose had met as children when their respective families were vacationing in Maine. They renewed their relationship in their late teens, fell in love and were married on 7 October 1914. Two of Boston's foremost families were thus united, although initially Honey Fitz felt that it was Joseph Kennedy who had made the better match. He would come to change his mind, however, when he saw what extraordinary talents his son-in-law possessed, and the singlemindedness with which he pursued his goals. Those objectives included becoming a millionaire by the time he was thirty-five, something he accomplished with room to spare.

Joe and Rose began their married life in a house on Beals Street, Brookline, a well-heeled - and Protestant - area of Boston. The latter fact was particularly significant, as Joe fought long and hard to gain the kind of social acceptance that he saw as commensurate with his status within the business community. He found that the Brahmins were quick to acknowledge him as a first-rate businessman, but they actively conspired to keep the Kennedys in the second division of Boston's social set. This rankled with Joe, who responded by adding to his wealth even more assiduously, which he regarded as the ultimate criterion. Joe's ultra-competitive spirit was instilled into all his children. Joe Jr, born in 1915, was the first to be imbued with the Kennedy mantra that it wasn't taking part that counted but winning. Jack was the second.

Jack was born in the year that the USA entered the First World War. His father didn't enlist. Instead, Joe accepted an offer to take over the running of the Fore River Shipyard in Quincy. His contribution to the war effort was typical of the Kennedy work ethic. Under his management production rocketed and he thus earned a bonus over and above the $20,000 salary that went with the job. Always with an eye to the main chance, Joe set up a highly profitable cafeteria for the 22,000-strong workforce, supplementing his income still further.

Shipbuilding was a temporary vehicle for Joe's

Opposite: Joseph Kennedy and Rose Fitzgerald, parents of the thirty-fifth president of the United States, pictured on their wedding day, 7 October 1914. The marriage united two of Boston's most eminent Irish-Catholic families.

skills. He had gone into the banking business after leaving Harvard in 1912. He didn't particularly distinguish himself in his studies. Finding outlets for his entrepreneurial ability was always far more important to him than academic achievement. His influence and connections meant that he went into the financial sector at a senior level, as state bank examiner. Even so, Joe's ambitions stretched far beyond that post, and to achieve millionaire status within the period he'd set himself there was little time to lose. After less than a year in the job he saw the opportunity he was waiting for. He borrowed to the hilt to take over Columbia Trust, one of the few financial institutions which wasn't hostile to the Irish community. It had been a takeover target of rival bank First National, but Joe held his nerve and won the bidding war. His reward was to be made president of Columbia Trust. It was put abroad that at twenty-five he was the youngest person in the country to hold such a lofty position. This may well not have been the case but it illustrated perfectly another Kennedy hallmark: knowing the value of slick self-

publicity, even if the facts failed to live up to the billing.

Joe later diversified into stockbroking, where he again displayed the Midas touch. This was partly down to astuteness and foresight, such as when he bought into movie theaters just when they were becoming the most popular form of entertainment. However, he was not above sharp practice either. A favorite trick, carried out with a select group of friends, was to generate rapid, high-volume turnover in a poorly performing stock. Unwitting investors invariably piled in, believing that the movement was indicative of a handsome return. But the only money to be made went into the pockets of Kennedy and Co., who sold their holding when the price had been pushed up far beyond its worth. The suckers, meanwhile, were left facing huge losses. Typically, by the time the market crashed in 1929, Joe Kennedy had liquidated his stock, adding to his fortune still further.

If Kennedy's stock market dealings were legal, albeit sometimes unseemly, then there is evidence to believe that he did indeed cross the line during the Prohibition era. He was said to have been heavily involved in supplying alcohol illegally until the thirteen-year ban came to an end in 1933. During that period he became involved with some shady characters, including mobster Frank Costello.

Joe's diversification into the movie business also provided ample opportunity for womanizing. He was a notorious philanderer, and although most of the liaisons were brief and casual, one nearly rocked the family to its foundations. Joe embarked on a passionate affair with the screen legend Gloria Swanson. At one point he sought dispensation from the church to be allowed to leave Rose and set up home with Swanson, but in the event the

Rose Kennedy with five of her children. Joe Jr (right) was born in 1915, with John (second right) arriving two years later. Rosemary, Kathleen and Eunice were born in 1918, 1920 and 1921 respectively. All the children were brought up with a fiercely competitive work ethic, though there was a particular rivalry between the two eldest boys.

The Kennedy family was completed in 1932, when Edward, known as 'Teddy', was born.

affair fizzled out acrimoniously. A disastrous project precipitated the split. The movie *Queen Kelly* was directed by Erich von Stroheim, who shot thousands of feet of film, much of it unusable due to its sado-masochistic content. Swanson finally walked off the set and washed her hands of the venture, only belatedly discovering that under the terms of her contract it was she who bore the chief financial burden, not Joe. She also learned that even some of the expensive gifts that Joe had showered on her had been charged to her own account .

Joe left the movie business having made another handsome profit, and drew back from the brink of ending his marriage. His eye continued to rove, but the family bond remained fixed and unbreakable. Rose accepted the status quo, as Jackie Kennedy would in similar circumstances a quarter of a century later.

By 1930, when Jack was entering his teenage years, Joe Kennedy had amassed such a fortune that he was able to set up a million-dollar trust fund for each of his children. They would not be allowed to rest on their laurels, however. The work ethic and drive to succeed instilled into all the children ensured there was no room for complacency.

There were now eight in the family. Rosemary was born in 1918, with Kathleen, Eunice, Patricia, Robert and Jean arriving over the next ten years. Edward was born in 1932. The ethos of the family took no account of gender, and the same tough, competitive streak was instilled into the Kennedy girls. Nowhere was this more apparent than in the regular games of touch football that the family engaged in. While all the children felt this competitive pressure, there was a particular edge between the two eldest boys. Theirs was a separate and constant battle of one-upmanship.

The one family member who struggled in this environment was Rosemary. She was born mentally handicapped and was eventually institutionalized.

Joseph Kennedy, pictured with his two eldest sons. Joe's hopes and expectations centered on Joe Jr (right), who was the undoubted star of the family.

The family closed ranks, both out of concern for Rosemary's welfare and to avoid the stigma which a public admission would bring. Joe in particular found it hard to come to terms with the situation, equating disability with failure.

Roman Catholicism was also central to the Kennedys' lives. Rose was devout, believing that religion was the glue which held every facet of an individual's life together. Joe was far more pragmatic. He knew that the qualities required to succeed might not always be in concert with the tenets of their faith. He paid lip-service to the church on Sundays, but for the rest of the week he did whatever it took to get the job done. When it came to sex and politics, Kennedy males would often find it expedient to relegate morality and piety to a convenient back burner.

Notwithstanding the privileges and comforts which the family wealth allowed, Jack Kennedy's early years were in many ways unremarkable. There were typical boyhood scrapes and pranks, and much greater interest in sports than studies. He had a tendency toward lateness and laziness. Both academically and in terms of sporting prowess, he suffered in comparison to Joe Jr. His older brother was at the head of the pecking order, the star of the family. Jack would live for many years in his shadow.

Jack's education began at the Dexter School, a private day school close to the Kennedys' Brookline home. In 1926 Joe moved his family to New York. He didn't want his children to face the same barriers he had encountered in Boston. He also felt New York would offer him greater opportunities to expand his business empire, and it was from there that he began commuting regularly to Hollywood. On the social front there was another early body blow, however, as he was blackballed from entry into the exclusive

Cohasset Country Club. As usual, Joe channeled his outrage into deal-making and wealth acquisition.

For Jack, relocating to New York meant a change of school. He became a student at Riverdale School, which was in the suburb where Joe had bought a house overlooking the Hudson River. Three years later the family were on the move again, to an eleven-bedroom mansion in Bronxville. Jack continued his education at Riverdale, but at the age of thirteen he was sent to Canterbury School, a Catholic boarding establishment in New Milford, Connecticut. It was the first time he had been away from home and no doubt was yet another stage in the character-building program that his father so carefully orchestrated.

Jack was an avid reader, particularly during the long periods of confinement he was forced to endure through a succession of illnesses. Unfortunately, whatever reading matter he absorbed failed to translate into academic distinction or even half-decent spelling. His strengths were undoubtedly his personal qualities: charm, wit and a well-developed sense of humor.

At Choate, a college preparatory school in Wallingford, Connecticut, the pattern continued in much the same vein. Joe Jr remained two years in front of him chronologically and streets ahead in terms of academic and sporting prowess. Jack graduated from Choate in 1935, when he was eighteen. There were times when it seemed he wouldn't survive in what was a seat of learning full of high-fliers. He did manage to knuckle down in his final year, yet it only pushed him up to a mediocre sixty-fourth in a year group of 112. Nevertheless, it was the personable young man who had scraped through who was voted by his classmates as the most likely to succeed.

Perhaps in an effort to assert his independence, Jack then opted to go to Princeton. Joe Jr, meanwhile, had followed in his father's footsteps and was already at Harvard in the summer of 1935. Jack traveled to England to study under socialist economist Harold Laski at the London School of Economics. Although the principles Laski espoused were anathema to the tycoon, he felt that an understanding of a left-wing economic perspective was important to provide a counterbalance to the wealth and privilege that capitalist America had provided. In the event, illness forced Jack to return home early and by the spring of 1936 he had had a change of heart. He decided that he did not want to take up a place at Princeton a year behind his friends from Choate. He would go to Harvard after all.

In his first two years at Harvard Jack again tried to match the sporting achievements of his older brother, but as ever it was a case of guts and determination rather than athletic ability. A severe back injury sustained during a football match ended his hopes of succeeding in that arena. It was something that would trouble him throughout his life. In true Kennedy style, however, he tried out for the swimming team instead. He also began to establish something of a reputation as a ladies' man.

Jack's political awakening now began to manifest itself. He had read Churchill's words on the growing Nazi threat; Republicans and Fascists were fighting for the soul of Spain, and at home Roosevelt was wrestling with the Depression. There was much to occupy the thoughts of a political science undergraduate. The ideas and principles which would shape JFK's political beliefs became further crystalized with a trip to Europe in summer 1937. In December of that year his father's political fortunes also took a turn for the better when he was appointed US ambassador at the Court of St James's. Joe was no ideologue or visionary. He felt the post was a long-overdue reward befitting the support he had given Roosevelt over two successful presidential campaigns. Neither would it have been lost on him that he would be rubbing shoulders with the king and queen of England and the country's aristocracy. It was a long way from the social exclusion he and his family had suffered at hands of Boston's Brahmins.

Joe took up the post in April 1938. The following spring, with Europe on the brink of war, Jack asked the Harvard authorities for special leave to go on a fact-finding tour of Europe on behalf of his father. He spent several months traveling around Europe and the Middle East. He used the information gathered as the subject for his final-year thesis at Harvard. Eventually re-edited and published under the title *Why England Slept*, the book became an instant bestseller. Almost inevitably, Joe had a hand in

Jack pictured in uniform before his discharge from the Navy in 1945.

value. At last Jack had found a sphere in which he eclipsed Joe Jr. That may have been merely a temporary state of affairs, but war was to bring a family tragedy and leave Jack as the sole incumbent of the starring role.

Jack left Harvard with an honors degree in political science in June 1940, when the Allied forces in Europe were experiencing some of their darkest moments. He briefly attended Stanford University's business school that fall, just as his father was returning from his ambassadorial duties in England. Father and son were as one in their view that America should maintain an isolationist policy. For Joe this meant an irrevocable rift between him and Roosevelt. Kennedy had finally decided to support FDR's bid for a third term in the White House, but when the latter was successfully returned, Kennedy resigned.

The USA's entry into the war was still a year away, but both Jack and Joe Jr enlisted before then. Joe Jr joined the US Naval Reserve and was posted to Squantum Naval Air Facility near Boston, where he began flight training. Jack should have failed any services medical on any number of grounds, but Joe pulled strings and his second son was assigned to Naval

the enterprise. He bought a huge number of copies in the first print run, ensuring widespread coverage for the work and an enhanced profile for its author.

Joe himself had been talked about as a future presidential candidate back in 1938, but that possibility receded quickly; he became a fervent isolationist, determined to keep America out of the war at all costs. There were allegations that he had made a stock market killing amid the political uncertainty, using privileged information to his advantage and there was also the matter of his continued womanizing. As Joe's own political fortunes were on the wane he was naturally keen to promote his second son's. As usual, Joe was less interested in the content of Jack's paper than its PR

Intelligence in Washington. Joe was initially fiercely protective of his sons and had not wanted them to risk their lives in a fight that was nothing to do with America. Now he backed them wholeheartedly, for war offered the two men the perfect opportunity to put all the Kennedy virtues into practise.

Jack was working at Naval Intelligence when Pearl Harbor was attacked, precipitating the USA's entry into the war. During his three-month spell in Washington he also played the eligible bachelor role to the full. One affair, with the Danish beauty Inga Arvad, nearly caused him a major embarrassment. She was under surveillance as a possible spy, and Jack's connections probably made the difference between being cashiered and quietly transferred. He was posted to Charleston, South Carolina, but the affair continued. Jack considered marrying the divorcée, provoking an angry reaction from his father. It was said to be the first major disagreement between the two men.

In the spring of 1940 Jack's back problem worsened and it was thought that he required surgery. He applied for a period of inactive duty, but the decision to operate was deferred. Jack reported to Northwestern University for officer training and there he signed up for PT boat duty. These eighty-foot plywood-hulled boats were fast and maneuverable but also notoriously unreliable and vulnerable. PT duty was regarded as highly dangerous, which made it a glamorous option for the likes of Jack, who longed to see active combat.

There was another reason for Jack's impatience to join the action. Joe Jr had just earned his wings and joined the Naval Reserve, an elite group. Jack would doubtless have seen PT duty as a way of redressing the competitive balance between the brothers.

He suffered a brief setback when he was kept on as an instructor after completing his training at Melville, Rhode Island. But in March 1943 he finally got his wish, with a little help from his father. Joe put a word in the right ear and Jack was soon on his way to the Solomon Islands in the South Pacific.

He was given command of PT 109, and in mid-July he was sent to the front line. Two weeks later, on 2 August, an incident occurred which became shrouded in mystery, one in which Kennedy was by turns both hero and villain. PT 109 was on patrol in Blackett Strait when it was rammed by a Japanese destroyer. The boat exploded and two of Kennedy's crew were killed instantly. Others were badly injured, including Patrick MacMahon, who suffered terrible burns. A small, fast, highly maneuverable PT boat should never have allowed itself to be hit by such a large vessel. Kennedy's leadership would later be called into question and he could easily have found himself on the carpet - or worse - for what was a uniquely embarrassing lapse. However, over the next five days he redeemed himself with acts of bravery which ensured the survival of the rest of his crew. In that time the hungry and

exhausted men made it to three islands, either by swimming or clinging to pieces of debris. Kennedy personally towed MacMahon for miles. He also swam out alone in dangerous waters when his men were securely ashore, seeking out an Allied vessel. Rescue finally came when they were spotted by some friendly natives, who reported their position to the Americans.

Kennedy was recommended for the Silver Star. The authorities chose to focus on the part he played in his crew's survival rather than any errors of judgment which precipitated the predicament. He eventually received the more modest Navy and Marine Corps Medal, but that didn't prevent Jack and his father making great political capital out of the incident in later years. With the passage of time the story became increasingly embellished, with many journals and biographies reinforcing the positive gloss.

The remainder of Kennedy's nine-month tour of duty in the Pacific was relatively uneventful. He returned to the United States at the end of 1943, his back problem becoming increasingly acute and spent the next six months with an easy posting in Florida. He fitted in a lot of partying along with his duties before finally being hospitalized for back surgery in June 1944. It was while he was recuperating from the disk operation that he learned of Joe Jr's death. Perhaps frustrated by Jack's celebrated exploits while he had been largely kicking his heels, Joe Jr had volunteered for a highly dangerous bombing mission. His aircraft was loaded with 20,000 pounds. of explosives and Joe set out for France, the objective being to knock out the V2 launching ramps. He was to bail out after setting the fuses, but the explosives detonated prematurely. He was twenty-nine years old.

The loss of the family's golden boy was a shattering blow and hit Joe particularly hard. By the time Jack was discharged from the military on health grounds in early 1945, the hopes and dreams Joe had harbored for his firstborn had transferred to his second. The mantle passed to Jack, who became only too aware of the level of expectation that now rested on his shoulders.

Joseph Kennedy at work as president of Columbia Trust, a position he achieved when he was just 25 years old. It was said he was the youngest bank president in the country, but Joe's ambitions were still not satisfied. He set out to achieve millionaire status by the time he was 35, something he accomplished with time to spare. On one occasion, a friend, noting Joe's seemingly unquenchable thirst for wealth and success asked him what he wanted from life. "Everything," came the reply.

Fitzgerald and Kennedy

Rose Kennedy's parents, John and Mary Fitzgerald. John Francis Fitzgerald was one of Boston's foremost politicians and an arch-rival of PJ Kennedy, Jack's grandfather. He was known as "Honey Fitz" for his smooth, loquacious style, and "Fitzblarney" became part of the local vernacular on his account. Rose was the eldest of their six children and father's favorite. Honey Fitz initially thought that Rose could have made a better match than to marry Joseph Kennedy, PJ's son. He would change his mind when he saw at first-hand what a shrewd operator his son-in-law was.

First tragedy

Left: Rose Kennedy nurses Rosemary on her lap, with Joe Jr (left) and John. Rosemary became the family's first tragic figure. Her intellectual development was impaired, and she became a fringe member of the family circle. Joe in particular failed to come to terms with having a child unable to compete and achieve.

Opposite: Joseph and Rose Kennedy's marriage survived many acts of infidelity. The most celebrated of Joe's affairs involved the silent screen star Gloria Swanson. When he invited Swanson to accompany him and Rose on a trip to Europe, the actress was left wondering whether his wife was "a fool or a saint".

Below: Brookline, Massachusetts, 1919. Joe Jr and Jack pose with their father on the running board of the family car. Having made a lot of money managing a shipyard during the war, Joe added to his fortune with stock market dealings that sometimes verged on sharp practice. He also diversified into motion pictures and the liquor business with equal success.

Rivalry and friendship

Right: Jack (pulling cart) with siblings (left to right) Kathleen, Rosemary, Eunice and Joe Jr. Along with Rosemary, Jack gave his parents most cause for concern as he was a very sickly child. Eunice was precocious and intelligent, while Kathleen was the most vivacious of the girls. Owing to Rosemary's disability, "Kick", as Kathleen was known, would assume seniority among the Kennedy girls.

Below: Athletic pursuits and a tight family bond were a feature of the Kennedys' upbringing. Rosemary, Jack, Eunice, Joe Jr and Kathleen, pictured at Hyannis Port in 1925.

Opposite: Jack and Joe Jr's relationship was one of fierce rivalry as well as fraternal friendship. During their formative years, Jack lived in the shadow of his older brother, both academically and in the field of sporting endeavor.

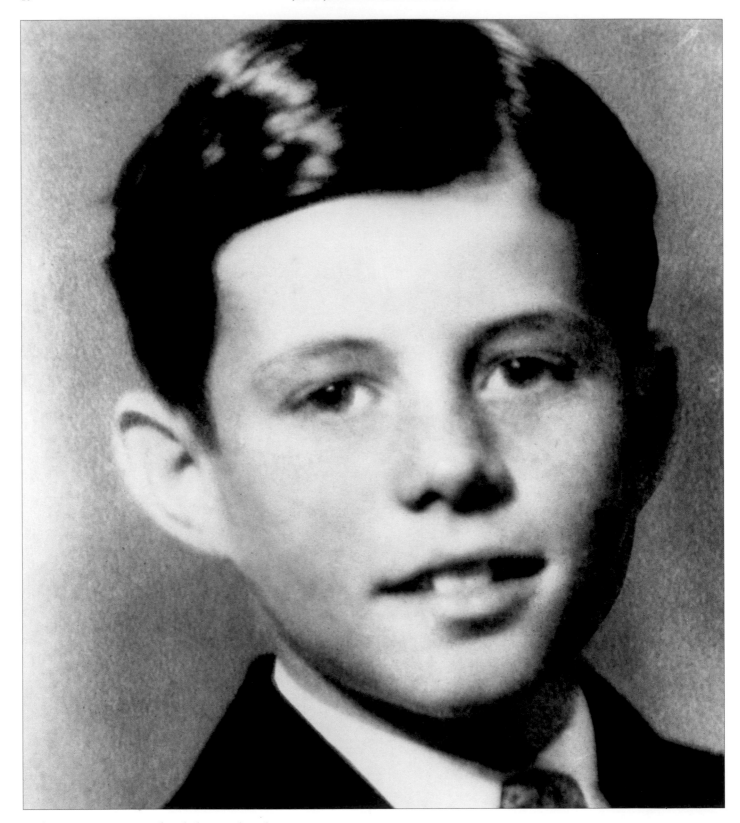

The unremarkable scholar

Above: John F. Kennedy aged 9. As a young scholar Jack lacked application and was a notoriously bad speller. He was also frequently in trouble for typical boyhood scrapes and misdemeanors However, during his long periods of confinement through illness he was a voracious reader, and books would be a lifelong passion.

Opposite: 10-year-old Jack sporting the footballing colors of Dexter School, Brookline. Jack's performances were notable more for endeavor than skill.

Turbulent childhood

Opposite: 12 August 1934. The Bouvier family attends a horse show at the Southampton Riding and Hunt Club, Long Island. Jackie's childhood was an emotional rollercoaster as the family home was a constant battleground. John and Janet Bouvier first separated in 1936, when Jackie was seven. After the marriage ended, she and her younger sister, Lee, went to live with their mother, with whom Jackie had a turbulent relationship.

Above: "Black Jack" Bouvier, immaculately attired as ever, walks alongside Jackie as she rides her pony. Jackie adored her father, despite the fact that he was vain, feckless and unfaithful. She admired the fact that he was a fun-loving reveller, and in her adult relationships she was drawn to men whose character had a dangerous edge. Jack Kennedy fitted the bill in this respect, and in some ways reminded her of her father.

"The architect of our lives"

Opposite above: With Joe Jr missing from this 1934 family portrait, Jack assumes seniority in the pecking order among the Kennedy siblings. But even as the children reached maturity the family remained patriarchal. All its members vied for the attention and approval of Joe Kennedy, whom Rose dubbed the "architect of our lives".

Above: The Kennedy family was completed with the birth of a ninth child, Edward, in 1932. The children were ultra-competitive, but were quick to close ranks against any perceived external threat.

Opposite below: Jack (standing third left) joined the Harvard Swim Team after a back injury ended his footballing days. Sports and socializing occupied a lot of Jack's time during his college years. However, his senior thesis on the the appeasement policy of the Chamberlain government in Britain during the late 1930s earned him great distinction.

The Ambassador

A family photograph taken at Hyannis Port in 1938. Joe Kennedy was appointed US ambassador to Great Britain that year. Rubbing shoulders with Britain's aristocracy appealed to Kennedy Sr, who had resented the social exclusion he had suffered at the hands of Boston's Brahmins. Even after Joe left office he liked to be known as "The Ambassador" for the status it conferred.

Jack's political awakening dated from this time, beginning with a fact-finding trip to Europe on his father's behalf.

The young author

Opposite: In the summer of 1937, the end of his freshman year at Harvard, Jack traveled to Europe with Lem Billings, a fellow student who would become a lifelong friend. In letters home Jack made some broad-brush observations about the political situation in Spain, Italy, the Soviet Union and England, but the trip was mainly for hedonistic pursuits.

Above: As usual, the sporting theme shows through in this family picture, with Teddy (kneeling) and Eunice (right) holding footballs. Missing are Joe Jr, Rosemary and Kathleen. Rosemary's absences were often explained away as "shyness".

Left: John, Robert and Teddy Kennedy, pictured at Hyannis Port. Bobby was an intense, gauche adolescent, lacking both the charm and magnetism of his two elder brothers. Teddy, the baby of the family, was a prankster and joker and much indulged by his siblings and parents.

Bound for Britain

Above: March 1938. Rose Kennedy and five of the children on board the SS *Washington*, bound for England to join Joe, the recently appointed ambassador. The two eldest sons remained at Harvard. Jack was in his sophomore year, while Joe Jr was set to graduate that summer. Rose was acutely aware of the importance of this diplomatic posting, both politically and socially. She had long harbored thoughts that Franklin Delano Roosevelt might offer the ambassadorship to Joe, and wrote to the president saying that the family were "honored, delighted and thrilled" at his decision.

Opposite: Jack vacationing in Cannes with Patricia (left) and Eunice. Eunice was intelligent and devoutly religious. Pat was widely regarded as the most beautiful of the Kennedy girls.

Bravado on the slopes

Patricia, Eunice, Robert, Joe Jr and Rosemary taking skiing lessons during a vacation in San Moritz at the end of 1938. Joe, Robert and Teddy all sustained limb injuries in quick succession as their natural bravado came to the fore. The Kennedys were by now a celebrated family on both sides of the Atlantic.

Fashionable society

Opposite: In early 1938 Joe and Rose took up residence at 9 Prince's Gate, the palatial embassy building donated to the US by philanthropist John Pierpont Morgan. They were quickly absorbed into fashionable society, with Rose showing far greater sensitivity to protocol than her plain-speaking husband.

Below: The Kennedys embraced London living wholeheartedly. Joe was keen to make his mark by helping shape US foreign policy; Rose organized the large embassy retinue and took a close interest in introducing her elder daughters into society; and the younger children all continued their education, with Rosemary placed at a Montessori school.

Left: Rose and "Kick", pictured at a society wedding shortly after the family's arrival in England. Kathleen's own romantic liaisons would cause deep divisions between mother and daughter.

High society

Above: London, April 1938. Kathleen and Bobby riding out on Rotten Row, shortly after their father's appointment as ambassador to Britain. Kathleen entranced a string of the country's most eligible bachelors. She would marry the man considered the most eligible of them all, Billy Hartington, son of the Duke of Devonshire. Rose Kennedy refused to give her blessing to a match between her daughter and a Protestant suitor, causing a rift within the family.

Opposite above: The ambassador returned to the United States briefly in June 1938, determined to further his twin ambitions: preventing his country from being drawn into a European conflict, while keeping one eye firmly fixed on the presidential election of 1940. He returned to Europe with Jack and Joe Jr aboard the SS *Normandie* at the end of June. Kennedy Sr set more store by doing than studying - as evidenced by his own Harvard days - and he wanted his sons to see politics in action at close quarters.

Opposite below: 11 May 1938. Rose is flanked by Kathleen and Rosemary as the two debutantes are presented at Buckingham Palace. Kathleen's natural charm and irreverence meant that she took meeting "George and Lizzie" in her stride. Presenting Rosemary at court was much riskier.

High-risk proceedure

June 1938. Joe Kennedy chats with Rosemary as they watch Bobby and Teddy officially open London's Children's Zoo. Rosemary adored her father, despite his coolness toward her. Joe was harsh about his eldest daughter's lack of intellectual capabilities, and was also critical of her tendency to put on weight. In 1941 he agreed to let doctors perform a prefrontal lobotomy on Rosemary, an experimental and highly dangerous proceedure. It made her condition even worse and she became institutionalized thereafter.

An independent view

September 1938. Jack returns to New York aboard the liner *Bremen*, after spending the summer in Europe. Three weeks after he returned to his studies at Harvard, British Prime Minister Neville Chamberlain emerged from the famous meeting at Munich declaring "peace in our time". Joe Kennedy, an admirer of the British premier, was elated at the news. Jack was more in sympathy with the views of Winston Churchill, who continued to warn of the threat posed by the Nazis. This was an early example of Jack exerting his independence.

Ambassador isolated

Above: Jack meets his father as the latter returns to the United States aboard the *Queen Mary*. Joe Kennedy became an increasingly marginalized political figure during his tenure as ambassador to Britain. President Roosevelt distanced himself from Kennedy, and there were soon calls for his resignation over his perceived compliant attitude over Nazism. He was also accused of anti-Semitism.

Opposite: The political science undergraduate took a six-month sabbatical from Harvard in the spring of 1939. He traveled widely in Europe as the continent was about to erupt into war, and used his experience as the basis for his final-year thesis at Harvard. Its theme was Britain's failure to prepare for the conflict, and it was eventually published under the title *Why England Slept*. Inevitably, Joe Kennedy had a hand in promoting sales of the book, buying up thousands of copies to ensure its success. He regarded a best-seller on a key political issue as a means of enhancing his second son's career prospects. The work was more noteworthy for Jack's increasing interest in international affairs than for any great insight into the political situation.

"Kick" and Marquess parted by war

Left: March 1939. Kathleen Kennedy and Billy Cavendish, Marquess of Hartington, at the Cambridge University Steeplechase. When war broke out and Billy received his draft papers, Kathleen wanted to remain in England. She was overruled by her father, who insisted that she return to America with the rest of the family.

Below: The Kennedy children, minus Joe Jr and Jack, en route to Rome for the coronation of Cardinal Eugenio Pacelli as the new pope, Pius XII. Rose's devout faith made this one of the defining moments in her life.

Opposite: Joe and Jack on their way to Rome for the papal coronation. There was a clear division between Kennedy males and females as far as adherence to their Roman Catholic faith was concerned. The girls fell under Rose's influence and were more devout. The boys took their lead from Joe, who was of the view that a weekly dose of piety was quite enough. The rest of the week was for the masculine pursuits of business and pleasure, neither of which was compatible with religious precepts.

Kennedys received by new Pope

Above: The Kennedy family are received at the Vatican. They had met the new Pope, Pius XII when, as Cardinal Pacelli, he visited the United States in November 1936. He had taken tea at the family's Bronxville home, and thereafter Rose had not allowed anyone to sit on the chair he had occupied.

Right: Jack's travels in the spring and summer of 1939 included a visit to Egypt. At this point Jack seemed to have the best of both worlds. He had rubbed shoulders with royalty and high-ranking diplomats, yet he was under no great scrutiny and had ample opportunity to escape from the spotlight. In one celebrated escapade in the south of France, he overturned his car on the way to a party and was lucky to escape serious injury. Jack was now comfortable in the role of number two son, which undoubtedly had its advantages.

Opposite: At a Fourth of July Garden Party, held at London's American Embassy, 1939. Jack dissented from the widespread view that Europe would erupt into war before the year was over.

Stars of the family

Above: Joe Jr, Kathleen and Jack, pictured in London on the day Britain declared war on Germany, 3 September 1939. Of the nine Kennedy children, these three formed a special group. Within a decade, Joe Jr and Kathleen would both be dead, leaving the focus of attention almost exclusively on Jack.

Opposite above: Jacqueline Bouvier, aged 10, at the Tuxedo Horse Show with her mother (right) and a family friend. Janet and her two daughters finally moved out of the family home at East Hampton in the summer of 1938. The couple were divorced in June 1940. The acrimonious split deeply affected Jackie, who developed the capacity to block out pain, something that would serve her well in later life.

Opposite below: July 1939. Rose Kennedy makes some last-minute adjustments to her daughter Eunice's gown before she is presented to King George VI and Queen Elizabeth at Buckingham Palace. 18-year-old Eunice didn't make the impact Kathleen had the previous year. She was clever and resourceful, but her dance card was often incomplete at the society balls.

"War would drain us"

Opposite: Joe and Rose Kennedy, pictured at their Palm Beach home in 1940. Relations between Kennedy and President Roosevelt reached rock-bottom late in the year, culminating in the former resigning as ambassador to Britain. With the death of Neville Chamberlain and the elevation of Winston Churchill to Britain's premiership, Kennedy's political isolation was complete. Free of the strictures of diplomatic office, he continued to voice his extreme opinions, commenting in one interview that "war would drain us" and "democracy is finished in England". His virulent anti-war stance had domestic roots too: he was keen to protect his sons from a battle he felt was nothing to do with America.

Above: Palm beach, 11 February 1940. Joe and Rose Kennedy celebrate Rose's father's 77th birthday. With Joe's political fortunes waning, the mantle passed to his eldest son. Joe Jr was a delegate at the 1940 Democratic Convention, although he needed his grandfather Honey Fitz to pull some strings in order to secure his seat. Influenced by his father, Joe Jr also adopted firm isolationist views.

Left: Eunice, Bobby and Jean, pictured at Palm Beach in January 1941. Jean, born 20 February 1928, was the youngest of the five Kennedy daughters.

Into battle

Above: Lieutenant John F. Kennedy was made captain of PT 109 in March 1943. Both Jack and Joe Jr signed up for military service before the United States entered the war. Jack's health problems may well have precluded him from active duty, but his father used his influence to ensure he passed the medical examination. Joe had initially wanted to keep his sons out of the war, but he came to regard the conflict as a vehicle for them to show their natural competitiveness and leadership skills.

Opposite below: Jack, pictured with some of his PT crew members. Paul "Red" Fay (right) became a close friend and served as Undersecretary of the Navy during Kennedy's presidency.

Opposite above: A family gathering at Palm Beach. The war years saw the family's three most charismatic members assert their independence. Joe Jr and Jack were both on active duty. Kathleen joined the Red Cross as a means of returning to England and renewing her relationship with Billy Hartington. The two would marry on 6 May 1944, with only Joe Jr representing the Kennedy family. Hartington was killed in action on 8 September.

The war hero

Above: At the helm of PT 109. Tours of duty in these plywood-hulled boats were notoriously dangerous. In the early hours of 2 August 1943, PT 109 was rammed by the Japanese destroyer *Amigari* in Blackett Strait in the Solomon Islands. Two crewmen were killed, while others were badly injured.

Opposite: In 1944 Lt Kennedy was awarded the Navy and Marine Corps Medal for his "extremely heroic conduct" after PT 109 was sunk. The award was for the valor and leadership Kennedy had shown during the five-day ordeal before the crew were rescued. The fact that he had been in command of a highly maneuverable PT boat when it was rammed by a destroyer was overlooked.

Decorated for bravery

Above: 13 June 1944. Lieutenant Kennedy is congratulated by Capt. F. L. Conklin after receiving the Navy and Marine Corps Medal. He was recommended by his commanding officer for the more prestigious Silver Star. After investigating the role Kennedy played in the survival phase of the incident, the naval authorities decided that the lesser award was more appropriate.

Opposite: Kennedy cuts a dashing figure during his naval service days. He returned from his nine-month tour of duty in the South Pacific a war hero, something he and his family would make much of during his political career.

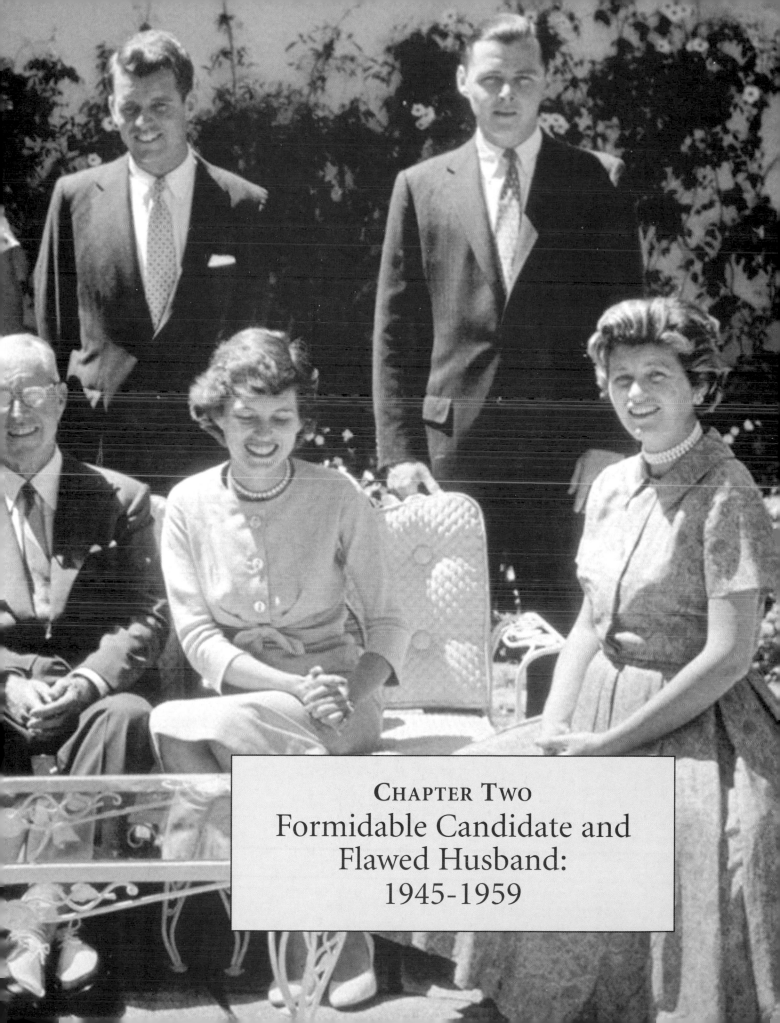

CHAPTER TWO
Formidable Candidate and Flawed Husband: 1945-1959

Jack had been considering several peacetime career options, but the pressure for him to make a name for himself in politics was overwhelming. Of course, the Kennedy machine would not let it be known that Jack had chosen this route by default. That would have smacked of a lack of conviction, passion and vision. And in the early days he was certainly no consummate performer on the political stage. He was not a natural orator, but his charm and magnetism were there for all to see.

Before he engaged in his first political battle, Jack spent some time working as a journalist. His father called in favors to secure him a job as a special correspondent for Hearst newspapers. He covered the Potsdam Conference, the first meetings of the United Nations and the general election in Britain. During the latter it is said that he predicted that Churchill would be comfortably returned when in fact the result was a Labour Party landslide. The pieces he wrote during his brief tenure as a journalist were of no great quality, nor did they offer any particular insight. However, they placed him alongside the most important movers and shakers in world politics and helped to raise his own profile.

There was a setback in August 1945, when Jack became violently ill during his visit to London. Details of his medical condition were rarely forthcoming, though it seems likely that on this occasion he had fallen victim to Addison's disease. This was a failure of the adrenal glands, the symptoms including weight loss and a yellowish skin pigmentation. He returned home, and with the war in Japan also now over following the dropping of atomic bombs on Hiroshima and Nagasaki, it was time to concentrate exclusively on mounting the first rung of the political ladder. Massachusetts was carefully targeted as the launchpad for Jack's new career. The Congressional seat for the 11th District was to be the first battleground. This was PJ Kennedy's and Honey Fitz's old stamping ground, and where his father had been born. Even so, allegations of carpetbagging were widespread.

James Curley was the target seat's incumbent but he vacated it in the fall of 1945 after winning Boston's mayoral election for the fourth time. Jack established residency in the city early in 1946, renting a room at the Bellevue Hotel. As the seat Jack was fighting was Democratic to the core, it was the primary that was the key vote. His early efforts out on the stump were not overly impressive. He worked hard on his speeches, practicing his delivery exhaustively, and there was considerable improvement. Even so, the campaign was based more on personality than issues. Jack even made a virtue out of being resolutely non-doctrinaire. If elected, he said he would simply tackle each issue on its merits. He was for jobs and against extremism, both of the left and right. It was all predictable fare. One cause which was close to his heart was housing, particularly for war veterans. Inevitably the recent conflict played an important part in the campaign. He gave a talk to Gold Star mothers, those who had lost a son in the fighting, and pointed out that his own mother was one of their number. And predictably, the heroic aspects of events involving PT 109 were kept in the public domain. The overriding impression was of a slick marketing exercise with Kennedy money liberally dispensed to oil the wheels. Some of this was handed out to individuals, ostensibly to cover any expenses they might

Opposite: John Fitzgerald Kennedy and Jacqueline Lee Bouvier, pictured at Hyannis Port two days before their wedding. It was the society event of the year.

have incurred or for any service they might have rendered. Political opponents complained bitterly that this was tantamount to greasing palms.

With the whole Kennedy family working feverishly in the background, the campaign was well-organized, polished - and successful. Jack beat off the challenge of the nine other Democratic candidates in the June primary, receiving twice as many votes as his nearest rival. And in November 1946 victory over the Republican candidate proved to be the formality everyone anticipated. Jack Kennedy, twenty-nine, had taken his first step to the White House.

Jack took his seat in the 80th Congress in January 1947, already tipped by many as a rising star. The fact that there was a Republican majority in both Houses made it even easier for an outstanding young Democratic congressman to catch the eye. At least it would have, had Kennedy shown any great talent or made his mark on the chamber. But having done what Kennedys were good at -

winning - the newly elected congressman exhibited little desire or interest in the affairs of state. He joined several committees, including the Education and Labor Committee, where he served alongside another new young congressman by the name of Richard Nixon, But he embraced no great cause, revealed no lively enthusiasm for the daily business of Congress. His attendance record was woeful, and although his continuing poor health was at least partly responsible, this didn't seem to keep him from his two other main interests, sport and socializing. If he displayed little passion for his professional duties, the same cannot be said for these extracurricular pursuits.

His peers, both political allies and foes, quickly got his measure. Many saw him as a lightweight, a lot of froth and little substance. Unsurprisingly, Joe Kennedy took a rather different view. He had staked a lot on his second son's future. The investment was emotional as well as financial, and Joe already harbored thoughts of a bid for the White House in 1960. With the ultimate prize as the long term goal, Kennedy Sr continued to keep close tabs on his son's professional and personal life, and Jack for his part continued to defer to his father's judgment on any number of issues. Many of Jack's contemporaries might have found Joe's lofty ambitions for his son laughable. The Kennedys knew that image was everything. In an era in which the media was burgeoning, JFK would be the first person to show that being photogenic and telegenic was a far more powerful political weapon than any amount of worthy, painstaking committee work on some minor bill.

In 1947 Jack embarked on a fact-finding tour of Europe. He fell ill in Ireland, where he had stopped off to visit his sister Kathleen. His condition worsened when he reached London, and hospital tests confirmed Addison's disease. He returned home immediately and last rites were administered. Later, cortisone treatment would keep the condition in check but Jack's political opponents would confront him with the truth on more than one occasion. Weakness was not part of the Kennedy vocabulary and Jack would continue to assert that his recurring bouts of illness were due to malaria contracted in the South Pacific.

In May 1948 the Kennedys were rocked by another family tragedy. Kathleen, known as "Kick", was killed in a plane crash along with her lover, Peter Milton, Lord Fitzwilliam. Kathleen had planned to marry Fitzwilliam, a Protestant and a divorcé. That was all too much for Rose, her wrath undiminished by the tragedy. She refused to attend her daughter's funeral. Jack, on the other hand, was distraught. "Kick" was his favorite sister and her death made him consider his own mortality. It also made him even more anxious to live each day to the full, and that meant an even greater turnover of women in his bed. His interest in the daily grind on Capitol Hill waned still further. This lackadaisical attitude was hardly conducive

Opposite: The young congressman, pictured with sisters Eunice (left) and Jean.

Below: Jack and Jackie first met in May 1952. There was attraction on both sides, but practical considerations also played a part in their decision to marry.

toward helping him fashion a political philosophy. Such minor details as lack of application and fixed beliefs didn't stop Joe setting in train the next upward move: the Senate.

In 1951 Jack traveled to Israel and the Far East, meeting such high-profile figures as Ben Gurion and Nehru. When he returned he spoke with gravitas on international affairs. One area of the globe that received particular attention was Vietnam. Jack had visited the country and was apprised of the conflict between the French colonial power and the Communist Vietminh. The defeat of the French at Dien Bien Phu was still three years away, after which the USA would become increasingly embroiled in Indochina. A decade after his fact-finding visit Jack would continue to wrestle with the same problems, only then it would be as president, not congressman.

Although Jack could now speak with some authority on foreign affairs, the Senate seat he and his father targeted for the 1952 election would be no pushover. The incumbent was Henry Cabot Lodge Jr, grandson of one of Honey Fitz's old sparring partners. He had been a senator for the best part of twenty years, in

which time he seen off many a Democratic challenge. Before he could take on the confident Cabot Lodge, it was necessary to secure the Democratic nomination. That cause was helped when Governor Paul Dever decided to run for another term in that office rather than try for the Senate. Joe Kennedy may well have had a hand in helping Dever reach that decision, one which left the way clear for Jack. The Kennedy machine swung into action. All the family contributed, with twenty-six-year-old Bobby cutting his political teeth as campaign manager. He carried off the role with ruthless efficiency, although it was Joe who was pulling the important strings offstage. The usual tactics were employed, focusing on Jack's youth, vitality and personality. His war exploits were revisited ad nauseam. Here was a man of principle and ideals, though he demurred from being too specific about any of them.

In a ceaseless round of tea parties and glad-handing, voters were treated to a seductive combination of Hollywood-style glamor and homespun homilies. There were two television debates in which Jack held his own against Lodge. With no great policy differences between the two it came down to image and presentation. That played to the Kennedy strengths and Jack duly won by 70,000 votes. The newly elected senator took his seat in January 1953.

Jack was widely acknowledged as one of the most eligible bachelors in the country, something he had played upon when pressing the flesh with the seemingly endless stream of young single women during the campaign tea parties. But by this time he had already met his future bride.

Jack first met Jacqueline Bouvier at a dinner party in June 1951. She was twenty-three, twelve years his junior, and had recently graduated from George Washington University. She was working as a photographer at the *Washington Times-Herald*. The Bouviers had been extremely wealthy. They had the class and bearing which the Kennedy family had long aspired to achieve. By the early 1950s the fortune had been largely dissipated but Jackie's cultured ways and breeding remained. She was also very beautiful.

Jackie had had a troubled childhood. Her mother,

Janet, and father, Jack, had had a stormy marriage. "Black Jack" was a feckless philanderer. Janet was naturally volatile and this fueled by alcohol meant the sparks regularly flew. Jackie and her younger sister, Lee, were not shielded from these domestic battles, and they had a profound effect on her. Jackie learned a cool detachment during this formative period. It wasn't her natural way to be unemotional and aloof but she decided early on that keeping the world at arm's length was the key to being more secure, less vulnerable.

Jackie was seven when her parents separated in 1936. Both children went to live with their mother. Jackie disliked Janet, who had regularly turned her guns on her eldest child to sublimate her anger with her husband. Jack, by contrast, was an indulgent father and for all his faults Jackie adored him.

Jackie's difficult relationship with her mother persisted long after the divorce from Jack and her remarriage to investment banker Hugh Auchinloss. Janet relentlessly undermined her eldest daughter, who

Opposite: The Kennedys were regarded as a golden couple when they married at St Mary's Church, Newport on 12 September 1953.

Below: Jack and Bobby were close politically as well as fraternally. In the 1950s Jack honed his political skills, while Bobby became a consummate organizer and fixer.

Above: Bobby, the younger brother by eight years, married Ethel Skakel (second left) in 1950. Ethel had much of the Kennedy spirit, whereas many of the family traits and pastimes left Jackie cold.

reminded her of her reviled ex-husband. Jackie became introspective and immersed herself in art, literature and history. In particular she had a voracious appetite for French culture, no doubt feeling a natural affinity to her father's roots. Janet felt that being intelligent and opinionated would be a handicap in landing a suitable husband, yet another source of conflict between the two. Her constant sniping took its toll, and Jackie suffered from low self-esteem. She deliberately adopted a kind of look, mannerisms and persona that her mother had convinced her men found most attractive.

One thing the two women did have in common

was an awareness of the need to make a good match. Janet discouraged her interest in one suitor, telling her she could do better for herself. She eventually became engaged to a stockbroker, a safe if unremarkable choice. But when the most eligible bachelor in the land began paying attention to her, the engagement was quickly called off. Jack's good looks, intelligence, charm, wealth and position naturally drew her to him. Even his playboy image was a positive boon, since it boosted the flagging self-confidence to know that such a desirable man was interested in her. For Jack's part, he thought her classy and erudite, as well as beautiful. That she was well read and had a passion for the arts and history were added attractions, not the handicap Janet had predicted.

Jack may have found Jackie interesting and attractive, but he was hardly besotted, and marriage was a huge step for a serial womanizer. However, Joe Kennedy thought a wife would be perfect for Jack's career, another part of the jigsaw slotted into place. Jack proposed in May 1953. Jackie was well aware of the number of women who aspired to become Mrs John F. Kennedy. Her initial response was to decamp with a girlfriend to London, where she combined sightseeing with work for the *Times-Herald*. Even so, her answer to Jack's proposal was not in doubt for long. He then promptly took off for a vacation in Europe. It was not to be a last fling, a final indulgence in the excesses of bachelorhood; fidelity was not going to be his strong suit.

They were married at Newport, Rhode Island on 12 September 1953. Naturally, it was a lavish affair, with Bobby doing the honors as best man. The newlyweds honeymooned in Acapulco and looked every inch a golden couple. The cracks began to show almost immediately, however. Jackie had a starry-eyed vision of becoming actively involved in her husband's work, a natural outlet for her intellect and curiosity. But she was to quickly reach the conclusion that politics was a tedious business. Even more worrying was the fact that her new husband wanted to have his marital cake and continue to dine as a bachelor. The ritual humiliation she had suffered at a mother's hands returned in a different guise, for Jack showed little discretion in his amorous pursuits. The same defense mechanism she had employed as a child during her own parents' bitter struggles again came into play. She became detached and aloof.

In mid-1955 the Kennedys moved into a $125,000 house in McClean, Virginia. With Jack absent for long periods Jackie devoted her talent and energy to a grand refurbishment scheme. Despite the Kennedy wealth, Jack was notoriously poor at handling money. He rarely carried cash, often borrowing from friends and aides when the need arose. Jackie's extravagant outlay on their new home, far from pleasing the senator, merely irked him.

The house move came as Jack was recovering from a major back operation. The highly risky double-fusion procedure had been carried out the previous October. An infection set in and he lapsed into a coma. Last rites were again administered. The subsequent convalescence was slow and painful. It was also notable on both personal and professional fronts; with Jackie in close attendance and philandering off the agenda, the marriage enjoyed a period of harmony and stability. Jack formulated his ideas for a book, *Profiles In Courage*, which documented figures in America's political history who had shown unswerving adherence to their principles, even in the face of adversity. He used Jackie as a sounding board and she also carried out research on his behalf.

Jack's incapacity also meant that he conveniently missed a key vote on one of the most controversial political figures of the day. Senator Joe McCarthy's notorious "witchhunts" against public figures who may have had Communist sympathies had become so extreme that the Senate decided to act. He faced a censure motion on 2 December 1954. Jack's stance on Communism was almost as fervent as McCarthy's, and he was also a family friend. On the other hand, Jack had the liberal wing of the Democratic Party to consider. He was still bed-bound when the vote was taken and used this as a convenient excuse for failing to register his vote. He was the only member of his party who failed to declare, and his opponents were quick to conclude that he ducked the issue. He did finally go on record that he would have voted for censure, but only some eighteen months later, when the heat had gone out of the affair.

1956 also saw the publication of *Profiles In Courage*. It was an instant bestseller and was awarded a Pulitzer Prize the following year. As well as lauding the achievements of an array of political heavyweights including John Quincy Adams and Robert Taft, the book also raised Jack's own profile several notches. The reader no doubt saw the author as a man of integrity and principle, someone who thought deeply about both his political heritage and the issues of the day.

Jack basked in the glory and kudos accorded him by the success of the book, although the integrity of the authorship was questioned. A key figure in both the research and drafting of the work was Ted Sorensen. Sorensen had joined Jack's staff early in 1953 when he was twenty-four years old. An attorney by profession, Sorensen had impressed Kennedy with his intelligence and painstaking attention to detail. He was also a brilliant speech-writer, and the combination of his prose style and Jack's delivery would prove to be a formidable weapon up to the presidential campaign and beyond. Sorensen's other main attribute was a fierce loyalty and he himself insisted that his boss was the sole author of *Profiles In Courage*.

1956 was also election year; Eisenhower was seeking another term and Jack was in contention as running mate to Adlai Stevenson. Stevenson had been roundly beaten by Eisenhower four years earlier and had major reservations as to whether including Kennedy on the ticket would help his cause this time around. Jack played down his chances. He said he was not seeking the vice-presidency, but let it be known that he would accept the nomination should it be offered. Stevenson was still unsure; despite his obvious qualities and appeal, Kennedy was seen by many in his party as young, inexperienced and lacking the intellect required for high office. There was also the question of his Catholicism. Regardless of the sentiments expressed in the Bailey Memorandum, a document penned by Sorensen to allay fears that a Catholic candidate would be a net vote loser, many influential figures in the Democratic Party thought the country was not yet ready for a Catholic on a presidential ticket.

In a move which stunned the delegates, Stevenson threw the choice of running mate over to the floor instead of naming his own man. In the ensuing vote Jack lost out narrowly to Estes Kefauver, the man whom Stevenson had beaten for the presidential nomination. Jack was gracious in defeat, outwardly at least. Behind the smiles of support for the Stevenson-Kefauver ticket he was hugely disappointed. Defeat was always a bitter pill for a Kennedy to swallow. The despondency wasn't to last long, however, as the Democrats crashed to an even heavier defeat than in 1952. Jack remained untainted by the Republican landslide of 1956, and in hindsight he came to view his failure to secure the vice-presidential nomination as a stroke of great fortune. It meant that he could set his sights on the 1960 election with a clean bill of health.

Jack ought to have been buoyed by the imminent birth of his first child. Jackie was heavily pregnant during the Democratic convention, but after losing out to Kefauver Jack sought solace and rest in a Mediterranean vacation. Jackie had already suffered a miscarriage, during their first year of marriage, and her doctor advised her against an overseas trip. Jack saw no reason to amend his own plans, and while he partied aboard his yacht, Jackie was sent to stay with her mother. They were still separated by the Atlantic Ocean when Jackie began to hemorrhage

and was rushed into hospital. An emergency Cesarean was performed but the child, a baby girl, was stillborn. Bobby hurried to his sister-in-law's bedside and two days later presided over the funeral. Jack had still not been located. When he was finally reached, he took the news calmly and saw no reason to return home. The fact that Jackie herself had been seriously ill in addition to the psychological impact of losing a second child seemed to elude him. It was a callous act and a watershed in their relationship. The humiliation of infidelity was one thing; surely this was beyond the pale. Ultimately, however, Jackie chose the status quo, with all the hurt and difficulties that went with it. She had once believed, or been led to believe, that men would not find her attractive. Marriage to Jack had briefly changed all that. Now that dream was well and truly shattered and Jackie, at least in part, blamed herself for her husband's dalliances. In short, the marriage wasn't perfect, it wasn't what she wanted or expected, but she decided to settle for it.

In 1957 the Democratic Party may have been licking its wounds from the previous year's electoral disaster, but for Jack Kennedy it was onward and upward. He had by now articulated his intention to run for president in 1960, and that meant four long years of exhaustive campaigning. Jackie had wanted to use her talents to support his bid, but in the event she remained a peripheral figure. There were two reasons for this: Jack's inner circle of advisers suggested that with her interests in highbrow culture and couture fashion, Jackie might be perceived as lacking the common touch and alienate swathes of ordinary voters; on a more practical note, early in 1957 she became pregnant again. It was a blessed event for both parents in more ways than one. Jack now didn't have to worry about a potential liability to the cause, while Jackie could make a dignified withdrawal from a political world she would come to disdain.

Caroline was born on 27 November 1957. Both parents were besotted with their baby daughter, although for Jack the way any event played on his image was never far from his mind. He was a doting father, and conveniently, that did nothing to harm his political ambitions. His philandering might have, had it reached a wider public. His sexual exploits were common knowledge on Capitol Hill and the press knew the score, but newspapers were not interested in a politician's peccadilloes unless they affected his ability to do the job.

Jack was constantly out on the stump, meeting and greeting, raising his profile and broadening his appeal. He was careful not to give his opponents the chance to stick a label on him. He wanted to garner votes from north and south, liberals and conservatives, Catholics and non-Catholics, black and white, and he thus nailed few colors to the mast. A notable exception was his work on the McClellan Committee, whose brief was to investigate corruption in the Teamsters Union. By taking on the powerful organization led by Jimmy Hoffa he showed that he was a man of courage who could play hardball when the situation required. Another area which he did revisit time and again in his speeches was foreign affairs, especially where there were implications for US defense policy. He spoke passionately about the political situation in Southeast Asia and ruffled many feathers with some trenchant views on France's bloody colonial struggle with Algerian nationalists. And then of course there was the Red Menace. Jack had long argued that the US was at

a military disadvantage to the Soviet Union, the famous "missile gap". His calculations could neither be proved nor disproved but they certainly struck a chord with those wary of a country which had already put the first satellite into space. In all these areas Jack spoke with conviction but there was a useful spin-off: holding forth on world affairs risked few votes at home and made him look ever more like presidential material. In his off-duty moments from what was an exhausting schedule he played hard, too, and was never short of female company.

1958 saw Jack up for re-election to the Senate, giving him the opportunity to check his progress. He was returned with 73.6 percent of the vote, the largest majority ever recorded in a Massachusetts election. Even before he had publicly declared his candidacy for the 1960 presidential election the momentum to carry him to the White House seemed unstoppable.

By mid-1959 the campaign was in full swing in all but name. A Corvair aircraft which was named *Caroline*

was purchased to make his constant criss-crossing of the country easier. It allowed him to reach more Democratic delegates and voters than any potential rival. The outlay was huge, but of course that was never an issue.

The schedule would have been daunting for a man in peak condition; for Kennedy it was all the more grueling. He suffered constant back pain, but at least the cortisone injections were helping to keep his adrenal deficiency under control. This treatment also fleshed out his face and made him even more handsome. Good looks cut little ice with some of the grandees of the Democratic Party, including Harry Truman and Eleanor Roosevelt, neither of whom thought he was up to the top job. They and many others underestimated the power of personal appeal; Jack and various family members were regularly photographed for glossy magazines. They were seductive images at a time when image was becoming increasingly important. As election year dawned, the Kennedy campaign rolled on like a juggernaut.

First steps on the political ladder

Above: Jack hosts a meeting of campaign workers as he bids to reach the House of Representatives in 1946. After the death of Joe Jr, Kennedy Sr made Jack's political career his number one priority. When the Congressional seat of Massachusetts' Eleventh District became vacant, Joe didn't hesitate. It was the old stamping ground of both PJ Kennedy and Honey Fitz, and he correctly calculated that a name with "Fitzgerald" and "Kennedy" in it, together with almost unlimited resources, would be a winning formula. The issues were unremarkable. Jack focused on matters such as employment and housing, with the welfare of war veterans always to the fore. But the main tactic was emotional: he sold himself as a war hero who offered youth and vitality.

Opposite: Relaxing at Hyannis Port after winning the Democratic nomination as congressman for Massachusetts' Eleventh District. As this voting area was overwhelmingly Democratic, the fall election was seen as a formality. On 5 November 1946, Jack comfortably beat his Republican opponent, the beginning of a 14-year journey which would end at the White House.

Joe Jr commemorated

Left: 12 August 1946. The Kennedy family marks the second anniversary of Joe Jr's death with a $600,000 donation to Archbishop Richard Cushing. The money was for the construction of a home for disadvantaged children, which would bear the name of the family's firstborn. Joe Jr had been killed when his plane blew up during a mission to destroy V-1 rocket bases in France. He had volunteered for the task, reportedly frustrated at his relative inactivity, especially compared with Jack's heroic exploits in the Pacific.

Below: The young congressman relaxes at his apartment in Georgetown, Washington. Initially, he shared the accommodation with his sister Eunice, who worked for the Justice Department. Having been elected to Congress, Jack showed little enthusiasm for the day-to-day affairs of government. His main reason for being there remained the fulfillment of his father's ambitions, not his own.

Opposite: Jack and Eunice entertained regularly at their Washington apartment. Jack's chief interests were still socializing and sports, and even allowing for his ongoing back problem, his attendance record in Congress was poor.

Family rocked by further tragedy

Left: 16 May 1948. Less than four years after the death of Joe Jr, the family was struck by another tragedy. Kathleen Kennedy was killed when a plane carrying her and her lover, Lord Fitzwilliam, crashed into a mountain near the town of Privas, France. "Kick" had gone to seek her father's blessing for her proposed marriage to Fitzwilliam. Joe, who was in Europe on a fact-finding tour for the Marshall Plan, was keen to find an accommodation to the problem. Rose was vehemently against the union, as Fitzwilliam was a divorcé. She had refused to attend Kick's wedding to Billy Hartington, and she would not attend her daughter's funeral.

Opposite: Jack and Franklin Delano Roosevelt Jr, who both took up the cause of war veterans' housing. In his early days on Capitol Hill Jack also served on the Education and Labor Committee, along with a young Republican congressman, Richard Nixon. Jack was non-doctrinaire in his views and he had many Republican friends.

Above: 24 August 1949. 20-year-old Jacqueline Bouvier (center) and some fellow students head to France for a year-long exchange trip. For Jackie the trip offered an escape from her mother, Janet, who was now Mrs Hugh Auchinloss. She was also drawn to the country because of her beloved father's Gallic roots.

Congressman on the march

Above: 18 April 1950. Jack is among a group of congressmen to accept a petition from a contemporary Paul Revere on the steps of the Capitol building. On the 175th anniversary of the famous midnight ride in which Revere warned of the coming of British troops, his latter-day counterpart petitions for home rule for Columbia. 1950 saw Jack returned to Congress for the third time. He deferred to the wishes of his father, who wanted him to run for the Senate in 1952.

Opposite: Joe and Rose Kennedy, pictured in January 1950. 62-year-old Joe was the power behind Jack's political career. He already had the 1960 presidential election in his sights, and kept close tabs on his son to ensure he did nothing to jeopardize that ambition. It was Joe who articulated the political advantages of Jack's marriage to Jacqueline Bouvier, and it was he who poured oil on troubled waters when the couple came close to separating.

Enter Jackie

Above: After graduating from George Washington University, where she majored in French literature, Jackie moved into journalism. After a brief spell at *Vogue*, she was appointed as the "Inquiring Camera Girl" at the *Washington Times-Herald*. She took up this undemanding job in January 1952. It was while working as a journalist that Jackie befriended Charles Bartlett, at whose house she first met Jack Kennedy.

Opposite above: Bobby Kennedy marries Ethel Skakel, with Eunice Kennedy (left) among the bridesmaids. Ethel had become Jean Kennedy's best friend during their college days at Manhattanville. Jean had played the part of matchmaker, pushing Ethel and her shy, awkward 20-year-old brother together during a skiing trip to Canada, Christmas 1945. The wedding took place at St Mary's Roman Catholic Church, Greenwich, Connecticut, 17 June 1950.

Opposite below: Eunice, Jean and Patricia Kennedy, who were bridesmaids at the wedding of their brother Bobby and Ethel Skakel. Ethel was wild and boisterous, and her tomboyish ways found favor with the Kennedy girls.

Slick campaign the key to Senate election victory

Opposite: Whenever possible, Jack sought to prevent his health problems from reaching the public domain. During the 1952 campaign for the Senate, his back pain became so acute that he was forced to use crutches. He often dispensed with them just before making his public appearance, but a lengthy session of speechmaking and handshaking sometimes made this impossible.

Above: Jack's 1952 campaign for the Senate was organized with military proficiency. His opponent for the seat was Henry Cabot Lodge Jr, grandson of the man who had defeated Honey Fitz in 1916. He too had looks, charisma and a fine war record. The difference was Joe Kennedy, who hired the best campaign team money could buy. The PR machine went into overdrive and Jack won by a margin of 70,000 votes.

Family out in force on campaign duty

Opposite: Pat and Eunice Kennedy go door-to-door to hand out car bumper stickers and photographs in support of their brother's senatorial campaign. All the family were mobilized, and in particular it marked Bobby's coming-of-age as a political fixer. When Joe Kennedy's strident and autocratic management threatened to demoralize the team, Bobby was persuaded to leave his job at the Justice Department and take over the running of the campaign.

Above: The senator-elect, pictured in November 1952. Jack held his own in two television debates with Lodge, and exuded charm and warmth which played well with the voters, particularly the young single females.

Gloom for Democratic Party, but not for Kennedy

Above: The newly-elected senator is showered in confetti as he arrives at his Boston campaign headquarters. This result was one of the few bright spots for the Democrats in what was a gloomy set of returns. The Republicans were in the ascendancy, both on Capitol Hill and the White House, where Dwight Eisenhower comfortably defeated Adlai Stevenson.

Left: 23 May 1953. Eunice Kennedy marries Robert Sargent Shriver at St Patrick's Cathedral, New York. Shriver had been an assistant editor at *Newsweek* when he met Eunice, and made no secret of his ambition to be a "right-hand man" to a top businessman. He was soon part of the Kennedy entourage, both as a paid executive and as a suitor to Eunice.

Opposite: Jacqueline Bouvier's elegance and beauty are captured in this 1953 portrait. In January of that year she attended President Eisenhower's inaugural ball with Jack. Having not seen him for several months after their first meeting in May 1952, Jackie was keen for the romance to progress. She knew the importance of making a good match and was aware that she had failed to "get the ring by spring" - the mantra of her college contemporaries to secure a suitable engagement before graduation.

"Most Eligible Bachelor" announces his engagement

Opposite: Jackie was well aware of Jack's playboy reputation during their courtship, but it only served to heighten the attraction. She was drawn by the element of danger that he represented, seeing shades of her father in his character and demeanor. Jack was taken by Jackie's cultured ways and witty repartee, as well as her beauty, although he was less than enthusiastic about the commitment of marriage.

Above: June 1953. The senator and his fiancée leave LaGuardia Airport to spend the weekend at Cape Cod. The engagement had been announced just after the *Saturday Evening Post* ran a feature on Jack as "Washington's Most Eligible Bachelor". It was a moment to savor for Jackie, whose mother had constantly undermined her and doubted her ability to attract a suitable husband. Jack, meanwhile, had no intention of allowing a marriage certificate to curb his bachelor ways.

Game, set, but no love match. Now 35, Jack realized that his father was right to suggest it was time for him to marry. Jackie intrigued him, he admired her intelligence, and he took the decision that this was enough for him to commit to marriage. The courtship was functional rather than romantic, Jack issuing his proposal by telegram.

Jack and Jackie, pictured at Hyannis Port two days before their nuptials. The Kennedy wealth was certainly an important factor in Jackie's decision to marry. Her father had squandered much of the Bouvier fortune, and when her mother married Hugh Auchinloss, she was surrounded by opulence but was made well aware that she would inherit virtually nothing. She had aristocratic bearing and a family name, but financial security was one of her overriding concerns.

Society wedding of the year

Opposite: 12 September 1953. Jack and Jackie take their vows at the century-old St Mary's Church in Newport, Rhode Island. Archbishop Richard Cushing, a long-standing family friend, came from Boston to officiate at the service, with Bobby acting as best man.

Left and below: A huge crowd of well-wishers amassed outside the church for the society wedding of the year. Jackie saw this day as more than just the beginning of married life. She was enthused at the prospect of playing an active role in her husband's political career.

Jackie's wedding day was marred by the fact that her father did not give her away. Informed by his ex-wife, Janet Auchinloss, that he was not invited to the reception, "Black Jack" got drunk and missed the ceremony. A devastated Jackie had to walk down the aisle on the arm of her stepfather, Hugh Auchinloss.

No one dissented from the view that Jackie made a stunning bride. However, she herself was less than pleased with her appearance. She disliked the ivory silk taffeta dress which her mother had picked out for her. The battle between the two thus continued right up until 24-year-old Jackie's wedding day. If Jackie thought that marriage would begin a fresh chapter of undiluted happiness, she was about to be disabused of the notion. The luster of the relationship began to wear off as early as the couple's honeymoon in Acapulco.

Family divisions

Above: The wedding showed up marked family divisions. Rose Kennedy and Janet Auchinloss engaged in a battle of wills over the arrangements for the big day. Janet wanted a more restrained affair, but the Kennedys insisted on a lavish celebration of their son's marriage. They agreed that the Auchinloss home of Hammersmith Farm would provide the backdrop, but new Kennedy money would pay for what would be a media event as well as a wedding.

Opposite: The newlyweds radiated happiness on their wedding day, but while Jackie embarked on married life full of romantic preconceptions, Jack was far more matter-of-fact about his new status. During their courtship he had written her a single postcard, bearing the words "Wish you were here, Jack".

Forced to miss McCarthy vote

Opposite: In October 1954 Jack's back problem became so acute that he was admitted to a New York hospital to undergo a risky double-fusion proceedure. The seriousness of the problem was kept out of the public domain. Any rumors regarding Jack's health were put down to infections and injuries sustained during his wartime service. The recuperation process afforded Jack an excuse to miss a key Senate vote, the censure motion on Senator Joe McCarthy. McCarthy had incurred the wrath of the Senate for his rabid anti-Communist stance and notorious witchhunts for those with "Red" leanings. Jack had a lot of sympathy with McCarthy's views, but also had to keep one eye on the liberal wing of the party. It was suggested that he could have made his opinion known but ducked the issue.

Above: Seven months after Jack and Jackie's wedding the Kennedys celebrated the marriage of Patricia to actor Peter Lawford. There were similarities between the two relationships. Like the Bouviers, the Lawford family had aristocratic roots but little money. Peter Lawford also felt the time was right to marry and was impressed by the status and wealth of the Kennedy family. There was no grand passion on his part, and the marriage would be dogged by acts of unfaithfulness on his side. Pat, like Jackie, had been concerned that the clock was ticking - she was nearly 30 - and was keen to secure a suitable husband.

Last rites administered

Below and opposite: Jackie and several family members are on hand as Jack leaves hospital two months after his spinal operation. Jack had lapsed into a coma after the complicated procedure, and last rites had been administered. When he left hospital, he faced a long recuperation. He had a raw, open wound, and Jackie played an important part in the recovery process, both psychologically and physically. His confinement, and thus his inability to be unfaithful, strengthened their relationship in the short term.

Left: A year into their marriage, the Kennedys present an image of harmony as they settle down to an evening of study after dinner. In fact, it had been a traumatic and revealing 12 months. Jackie suffered a miscarriage which, in a family known for its fecundity, inevitably meant a sense of failure as well as loss. Jackie's excessive spending annoyed Jack, who was notoriously careful with money. The new Mrs Kennedy realized that she was not to play a full supporting role in her husband's political life, and she also found that Jack had merely paid lip service to the idea of marital fidelity.

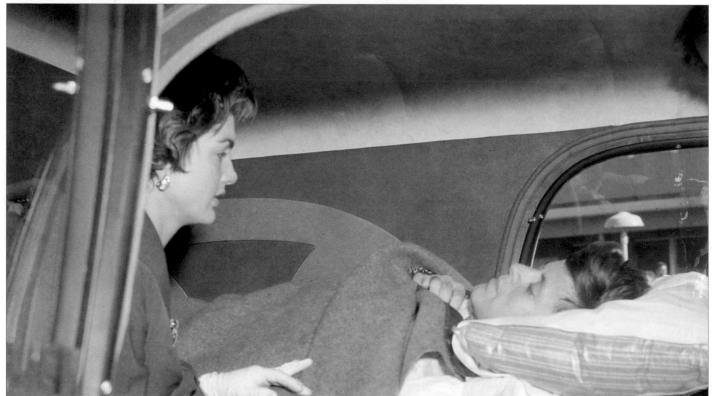

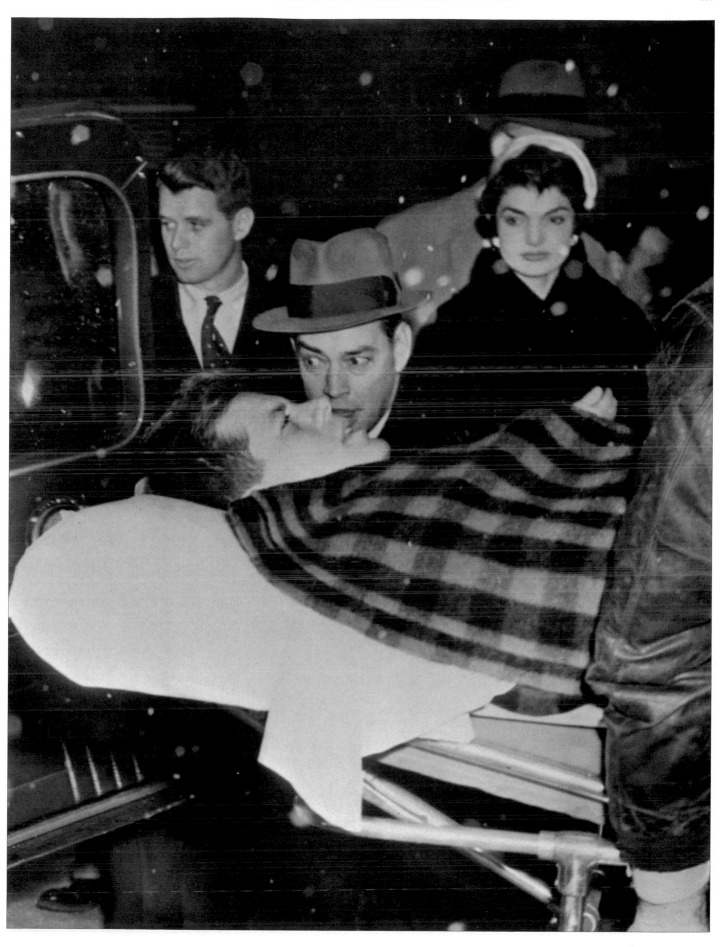

Pulitzer Prize for *Profiles In Courage*

Above: Jack and Jackie enjoy an evening at the Stork Club in May 1955, the month the senator returned to Capitol Hill after his long recuperation from back surgery. During his recovery, Jackie had helped her husband put together ideas for a book about eight senators who had shown outstanding political bravery. It was published early the following year to great acclaim under the title *Profiles In Courage*. The book won a Pulitzer Prize, and enhanced Jack's reputation as a deep political thinker.

Opposite: In October 1955 the Kennedys returned from a nine-week tour of Europe, which included visits to NATO countries and Communist Poland. Jack's weight had dropped to 140lb during the previous year. He was now being prescribed Novocaine and cortisone, and the latter also had the effect of fleshing out his face. The thin, somewhat gaunt look was gone for good, something which appealed to Jack's vanity.

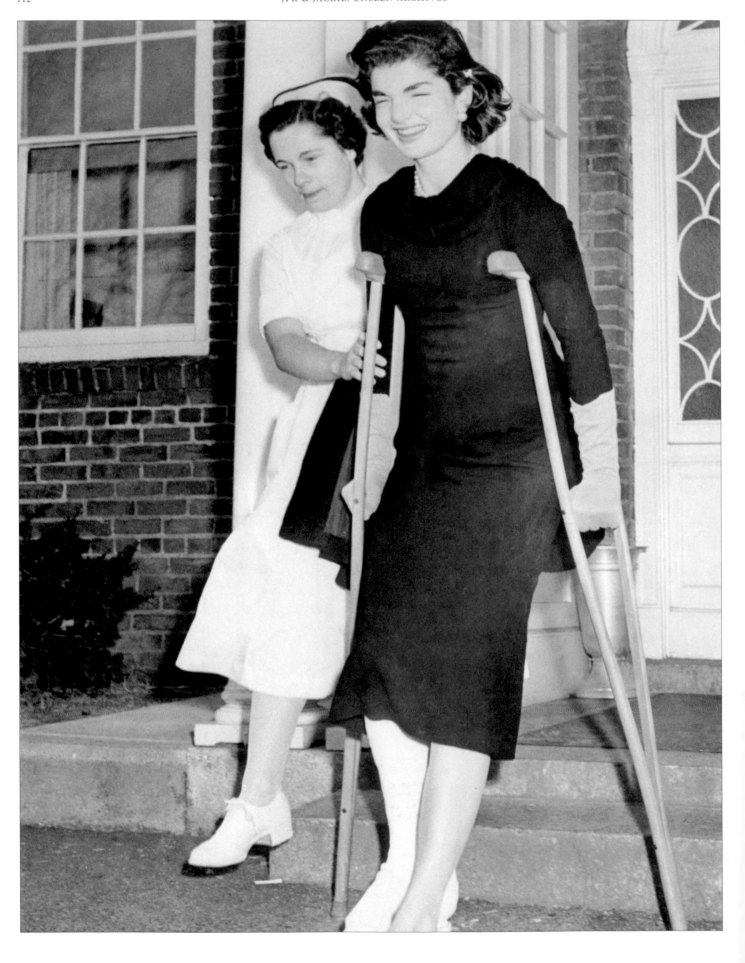

"The Deb" sustains football injury

Opposite: Jackie tried to embrace the Kennedys' love of competitive sports. A broken ankle while playing touch-football at Cape Cod ended her participation in an activity for which she had no enthusiasm.

Above: Jackie called her sisters-in-law the "Rah-Rah Girls" or "Toothy Girls". They dubbed her "The Deb", and took to mimicking her high-pitched voice. The occasion was a party to celebrate Jean Kennedy's engagement to Stephen Smith. (Left to right) Jackie Kennedy, Patricia Lawford, Ethel Skakel Kennedy, Jean Kennedy, Eunice Shriver.

Left: Joe and Rose Kennedy with their daughter Jean on her wedding day, 19 May 1956. Joe offered Jean the choice between a large wedding and a large present. Jean opted for a beautiful diamond brooch and a more modest wedding. Her husband, Stephen Smith, like so many others who married into the Kennedy family, was subsumed into it. He left his family's transport business to become yet another cog in Jack's campaign team.

Missing out on vice-presidency a hidden blessing

Opposite above: Eunice Shriver and Jackie at the Democratic Convention, Chicago, 13 August 1956. Jackie was eight months pregnant at the time. Despite the fact that she had already suffered a miscarriage, Jack headed off to the Mediterranean after the Convention. While he partied, Jackie was dispatched to Hammersmith Farm to stay with her mother. She went into premature labor and bore a stillborn child while Jack was on vacation. When he was finally contacted, Jack saw no reason to return home.

Opposite below: 16 August 1956. Jack is widely acclaimed for a barnstorming speech in which he nominated Adlai Stevenson as the Democratic Party's presidential candidate. He went to the Convention insisting he was not a candidate, but let it be known that he would accept the nomination as Stevenson's running mate should it be offered. Stevenson stunned delegates by throwing the choice of vice-president over to the floor, and in the subsequent vote Jack lost out to Estes Kefauver.

Above: Teddy, Jack and Bobby share a joke in an off-duty moment in 1956. It was a pivotal year for Jack. His failure to secure the vice-presidential nomination turned out to be a blessing in disguise. The Adlai Stevenson-Estes Kefauver ticket was trounced in the November presidential election. Jack's stock had risen during the Convention, yet he remained untainted by the crushing electoral defeat.

A family portrait, 1st January 1957. The women who married into the Kennedy clan quickly learned that it was patriarchal, with Joe at the undisputed head of the family. Kennedy males took precedence in the pecking order, irrespective of age.

The new year brought with it a fresh resolve. Jack and Jackie's marriage had come close to breaking point in 1956, not least because of Jack's callous treatment of Jackie over the birth of a stillborn child. Joe Kennedy had fulminated at the idea of divorce, drawing a parallel between his decision to put his marriage before Gloria Swanson nearly 30 years earlier. Politically, father and son were now as one as far as running for the presidency in 1960 was concerned. The decision was not made public, but unofficially the campaign was under way.

Following pages: February 1957. Jack and Bobby confer during a meeting of the McClellan Committee, which was investigating corruption within labor organizations. Jack served on the committee, whose main target was the powerful Teamsters Union, led by Dave Beck and his deputy, Jimmy Hoffa. Bobby served as Chief Counsel to the committee. He flourished in a two-year period of painstaking investigative work, particularly his personal duel with Hoffa.

Bobby takes on Hoffa

Above: Jack and Bobby in pensive mood during the McClellan Committee hearings. Jimmy Hoffa, who succeeded Beck as leader of the Teamsters Union, had been the subject of investigations as early as 1951. Joe Kennedy was wary of taking on such powerful vested interests, and the Democratic Party had traditional links with organized labor. Jack also had reservations, but Bobby was determined to bring to book those responsible for corrupt practices. Once the investigations were under way, Jack began to see - and reap - the political benefit of being associated with the committee's crusading work.

Opposite: The McClellan Committee was wound up in 1959. Those under investigation regularly "took the Fifth" and opposition from Republicans on the committee also made it difficult to secure indictments. When Jack became president and Bobby was head of the Justice Department, the two would renew their fight against organized crime.

April 1957. The Kennedys and Eunice Shriver attend the "April in Paris" Ball at the Waldorf-Astoria, New York. The early months of 1957 had been momentous for Jackie. She decided not to seek a divorce. The hopes with which she had begun married life had been dashed, but she decided to settle for what it offered. She also intended to play an active role in support of Jack's presidential campaign. Those plans had to be drastically scaled back when she found she was pregnant for the third time. Both Jack and Jackie were secretly pleased that she would be a peripheral figure in the campaign. Jackie found the endless speechmaking and glad-handing tedious, while Jack thought that his wife's refined tastes and designer clothes might deter some voters.

Jackie gives birth to a daughter

Above: After two pregnancies which ended in tragedy, Jackie gave birth to a daughter on 27 November 1957. The child was named Caroline Bouvier, after Jackie's sister - whose full name was Caroline Lee - and her father. Black Jack had died from cancer the previous August. Jack was besotted by his daughter, a complete transformation from the indifference he had shown following Jackie's two previous pregnancies. Although fatherhood didn't curb Jack's philandering, it did strengthen the bond between mother and father.

Opposite: Jack shows off a broom-shaped pin on his lapel, indicating the hopes of the Democratic Party for a "clean sweep" in the 1958 elections. Jack's re-election to the Senate was hardly in doubt, but the family were looking for an overwhelming majority to gain an unstoppable momentum that would carry Jack all the way to the White House. In the event, he took over 73 percent of the vote, the largest majority ever recorded in a Massachusetts election. Jackie played an active role in the campaign, and deliberately toned down her apparel to give the impression that she was in tune with the ordinary voter.

A family bond, a media circus

Above: Jackie regarded becoming a mother as the happiest day of her life. It ended all the doubts about her ability to carry a healthy child to term, and it meant that she and Jack now had the bond of parenthood. Jackie tried to protect Caroline from the inevitable media interest, although she did allow *Life* magazine to do a photo-shoot in 1958, when Jack was running for re-election to the Senate. Jack was rather more relaxed about using family shots for PR purposes.

Opposite below: Bobby Kennedy, pictured with some of his children in June 1957. By the time Jackie lost her second child in 1956, Bobby and Ethel had already produced five children in six years. Jack decided to sell his and Jackie's home, Hickory Hill, to his brother and sister-in-law, who needed more space for their growing family.

Opposite above: Ethel Kennedy, Jean Smith and Eunice Shriver look on anxiously as Jack and Bobby continue their probe into union racketeering on the McClellan Commitee. Eunice was articulate and politically astute, and only her gender relegated her to a supporting role in the campaign team.

Above: Jack and Bobby, pictured shortly before the campaign team was officially assembled, in the fall of 1959. The Kennedys were quick to grasp that the messenger was as important as the message, if not more so. In a country that was accustomed to hard sell, they understood that a presidential candidate could be marketed and sold like any other product.

Opposite: Jack and Jackie's leisure interests were quite different. Jackie, an expert horsewoman, loved country pursuits, including hunting. Jack was happiest when he was messing around in boats.

CHAPTER THREE

President-elect: 1960

Jack Kennedy formally announced his candidacy on 2 January 1960. The themes of his address were the arms race and the Soviet threat, managing the newly emerging nations, and creating the conditions for prosperity at home. A moral imperative would inform all policy matters in a Kennedy administration. It was motherhood and apple pie; there was nothing that anyone could take exception to.

He announced his intention to enter several primaries, hoping to overwhelm his potential rivals. Chief among these was Hubert Humphrey. The Minnesota senator went head-to-head with Jack in the Wisconsin primary, and quickly felt the full force of the Kennedy machine. By comparison he had meager resources, not to mention a less glamorous consort. Jackie played the role of the dutiful candidate's wife to the full, and the pair worked the crowds like Hollywood stars. Pregnancy would soon force Jackie to take a back seat, something which, no doubt, she was not too unhappy about.

Jack won in Wisconsin, taking 40 percent of the popular vote. He and Humphrey then moved on to West Virginia, which would prove to be decisive as far as the latter's chances were concerned. Religion quickly emerged as a key issue; there were undoubtedly voters who would find it difficult to stomach a Catholic in the White House. Jack decided to go on the offensive. He stressed his view that a clear line be drawn between church and state - religious beliefs would play no part when it came to making

Opposite: Jackie put aside her disdain for politics to play an active role in the campaign until pregnancy forced her to take a back seat. During the primaries, Hubert Humphrey acknowledged that the "Jackie factor" contributed towards his defeat.

policy. The trump card was his and his elder brother's wartime service. He pointed out that Uncle Sam hadn't been interested in their religion when the two of them had gone into battle. This was a persuasive argument, and it had the secondary effect of bringing Humphrey's own war record into play. Humphrey had been unfit for active service. It was all perfectly genuine, but it looked poor next to the resumé of a decorated war hero.

Humphrey could hardly have wanted any more bad news, yet it also became clear that some of his natural supporters switched sides merely to avoid being labeled bigots. Others disregarded the issue altogether, having had a positive experience of Catholics in positions of political power over many years.

The Kennedys left nothing to chance. Franklin Delano Roosevelt Jr was brought into the campaign team, a clever move which gave the illusion that one of the hallowed names in US political history was supporting the Kennedy campaign. They would hardly have asked Eleanor Roosevelt to bat for the team. She had no time for Kennedy, and once famously remarked that he had often showed "too much profile and not enough courage". Issues such as the McCarthy censure motion and civil rights had prompted the former First Lady's acidic comment, turning the Pulitzer Prize-winning work back on its author.

Notwithstanding Eleanor Roosevelt's criticisms, the mood of the majority in West Virginia was clear: here was a man who could prevent the Republicans from making it a hat-trick of victories in presidential elections. Jack carried the state by 219,000 to 142,000 votes, taking 61 percent of the popular vote. Humphrey, tearful and bitter, withdrew from the race. He pointed to the amount of money that his opponent was able to throw at the campaign as the decisive factor. It later emerged that some of those vast resources were used for dubious purposes. Large donations were made to Protestant ministers, and years later some openly admitted that this thinly veiled bribery had had the desired effect when it came to the ballot box.

Amid all the hectic politicking there was still time for affairs. One such, with Judith Campbell, was the most blatant yet, particularly in light of the intense media scrutiny he was under as the front-running candidate. It

was also potentially the most explosive. The two met in March 1960, a matter of weeks into Jackie's latest pregnancy. They were brought together by Frank Sinatra, and the entertainer also introduced Campbell to another of his associates, Mafia boss Sam Giancana. Far from recoiling at the prospect of sharing a mistress with a mobster, especially at such a sensitive time, Jack seemed to welcome it. He persuaded Campbell to arrange a meeting between him and Giancana, which took place in mid-April. There was certainly a rapprochement thereafter, with the Mafia heavily involved in getting the Kennedy

Opposite: Jack and Bobby talk tactics in the run-up to the Democratic convention. The two worked in tandem when the civil rights issue threatened to derail the campaign. Jack made all the right liberal noises in public, while Bobby wooed Southern delegates behind the scenes.

Above: The camera loved Jackie. She spent an inordinate anount of time on her appearance, which caused friction between her and Rose Kennedy. She also spent a huge amount of money on her wardrobe, which Jack feared might have political consequences.

vote out by any means at their disposal. Giancana was undoubtedly seeking influence at the highest level and an accommodation regarding federal probes into Mafia business.

Back on the campaign trail, there was a bandwagon effect which made it difficult to see beyond Jack Kennedy as the Democratic presidential candidate. He comfortably prevailed in several other primaries, and the more he looked like a winner, the more the voters swung behind him. By July 1960, when Los Angeles hosted the Democratic convention, there seemed to be only one

final hurdle to overcome. Lyndon Johnson belatedly threw his hat into the ring. The veteran Senate majority leader made much of his greater experience. He had put in the time, making a major contribution to the legislative program while his opponent had busied himself on peripheral matters, when he could be bothered to turn up at all. Jack responded by making a virtue of his youth and vitality; this was an obvious sideswipe at the major heart attack Johnson had suffered five years earlier. In turn, Johnson's camp brought up the question of Jack's own continuing health problems. LBJ fulminated over this "scrawny" specimen who was himself at death's door. It threatened to get very nasty indeed.

Jack had done a lot to keep the conservatives on board, particularly with his hard-line anti-Communist stance. He needed to boost his liberal credentials, and the civil rights issue gave him the perfect platform. He hadn't been outspoken on the subject until now, but in the final days leading up to the vote he went into overdrive. Johnson's last throw of the dice was to challenge Jack to a television debate, where he hoped his greater experience would give him the edge. But Jack was too wily for that; he kept on safe ground, spoke in broad generalities and it proved inconclusive.

Jack won the nomination on the first ballot, with 806 votes to Johnson's 409. Despite the animosity between the two men, Jack chose Johnson as his running mate, a decision which initially shocked his campaign team. It was a pragmatic decision on both sides. Jack knew that with the Texas man on the ticket the party would fare better in the vital Southern states. He also thought it better to have Johnson on board rather than relegate him to the role of hostile outsider. Besides, there was every chance that LBJ would throw the offer back in his face. Johnson didn't. He wanted the top job, and is said to have reached his decision after counting up the number of presidents who had died in office.

In his acceptance speech Jack spoke of the "new frontier", with echoes of Roosevelt's famous New Deal nearly thirty years earlier. He said: "There are new frontiers for America to conquer, in education, in science, in national purpose. Not frontiers on a map, but frontiers of the mind, the will, the spirit of man".

The man who stood between Jack and the White House was Eisenhower's vice-president, Richard Nixon. Nixon's legacy from Eisenhower was prosperity at home and peace abroad, and he began the campaign ahead in the polls. After Congress was adjourned on 1 September , Jack hit the ground running to make up the deficit. Over the next two months he made countless five-minute speeches, with overcoming inertia as a recurring theme. He would get America moving again, moving forward. The religious question came up again, more often than not at Kennedy's request. Nixon wanted it off the agenda, but Jack saw the value of raising the issue in order to dismiss it.

The highlight of the campaign was a series of four televised debates between candidates. The first, on 26 September, proved to be the watershed. The content of the debate was unremarkable, but this was to be all about image. The camera loved Jack, while Nixon, with his sweating brow and five-o'clock shadow, looked ill at ease. Those who listened to the debate on radio found Nixon's authoritative, resonant voice more appealing, and felt he got the better of the exchanges. But they were in a minority compared to the seventy million who had the pictures to go with the words. Afterwards, when Kennedy was out on the stump he was mobbed like a movie star. Even Nixon himself would later acknowledge that Kennedy's looks and charisma were major factors in determining the outcome of the election.

Victory was now in Jack's hands. It would take a seismic event for Nixon to turn things round in the remaining weeks until polling day. One such event did occur, but Nixon failed to take advantage. It concerned Martin Luther King, the thirty-one-year-old head of the Southern Christian Leadership Conference and the most prominent black leader in the country. King was jailed on 19 October for taking part in a sit-in in Atlanta, protesting about the city's segregationist practices. A trumped-up driving charge was added to King's minor misdemeanor and he was sentenced to four months in jail. While Nixon wavered, Kennedy aides suggested that Jack make a direct call to King's wife, Coretta, expressing his concern. Bobby made representations to the judge, and King was released soon afterwards. King had been a lukewarm Kennedy supporter before the incident; now he openly endorsed the Democratic candidate, and at a stroke virtually assured Jack of carrying the majority black vote. One of those was King's own father, an avowed Republican.

On 8 November Jack, accompanied by Jackie, cast his vote from 122 Bowdoin Street, Boston, the address he had maintained since he first ran for Congress. In the event it proved to be a very close-run thing. More than sixty-eight million votes were cast, the biggest turn-out in the country's history. Just 112,000 votes separated the candidates, the closest result since 1884, when the electoral roll was obviously considerably smaller. The margin of victory in the Electoral College was more decisive, Kennedy securing 303 votes to Nixon's 220.

On the morning of 9 November, John Fitzgerald Kennedy made his acceptance speech at Hyannis Port Armory. At forty-three he was the youngest-ever elected president and the first Catholic incumbent. The election machine had done its job; it was now time to see what Kennedy would deliver in office.

First, however, there was a family celebration. On 25 November three weeks after the election, Jackie gave birth to their second child. Jack missed the birth yet again, though his attitude was far less cavalier this time. He was en route to Florida when he learned that Jackie had been taken to hospital. He made every effort to return to Washington in time, but John F. Kennedy Jr had already been delivered by Cesarean section. If Jackie entertained hopes that fatherhood the second time around and the responsibilities of office would put a brake on Jack's tendency to wander, she was to be sorely disappointed.

Below: Jack realized his looks and style were perfectly suited to television. After the four televised debates with Nixon, Kennedy sought a fifth. Unsurprisingly, Nixon declined.

SENATOR JOHN F. KENNEDY
PRESIDENTIAL CANDIDATE

Cronkite interviews the declared candidate

Above: Legendary CBS news anchorman Walter Cronkite prepares to interview Kennedy. Jack formally declared that he was running for president on 2 January 1960, although in reality he had been campaigning non-stop since the Senate elections of 1958. It was the start of the year which would be the culmination of a 14-year journey since Kennedy entered politics. For his father it would be the realization of a dream. Cronkite raised the Catholic issue during the discussion, despite an agreement that religion was to be off-limits.

Left: Jack's political opponents bemoaned the effect that both Jackie and Caroline had on public opinion. The candidate encouraged family photo-opportunities to capitalize on the fact. He named the Corvair aircraft purchased for electioneering purposes after his daughter.

Opposite: Jackie and Caroline wait for Jack to fulfill yet another speaking engagement. Jackie was portrayed as a full-time mother, yet she employed a live-in nurse to cater for Caroline's everyday needs.

Kennedy targets primaries

Above: On the stump with Jackie in Nashua, New Hampshire, 25 January 1960. Despite his obvious appeal, Jack faced three major handicaps in winning the Democratic presidential nomination. He was young and relatively inexperienced, especially compared with Lyndon Johnson, who was seen as a likely rival; accusations were still rife that he was not his own man but a mere pawn acting out his father's own thwarted ambitions; and there was the issue of his faith, no Roman Catholic ever having been elected as chief executive of the United States. Jack took the decision to enter several primaries, hoping to build up momentum in his bid to become the Democratic presidential candidate. He carried New Hampshire comfortably.

Opposite: Many senior figures in the Democratic Party, including Harry Truman and Eleanor Roosevelt, thought that Kennedy had too much image and too little substance. They underestimated the power of personal appeal and charisma, which Kennedy had in abundance.

Humphrey's hopes ended

Right: Pressing the flesh in Charleston, West Virginia. Jack took 61% of the popular vote in the state, effectively ending Hubert Humphrey's chances of securing the Democratic nomination.

Above: Jack attends the 309th commencement of Harvard University. He was a Harvard alumnus himself, graduating cum laude in political science in 1940.

Opposite above: Jack is guest of honor at the Massachusetts Pre-Preliminary Convention dinner in Boston. State Secretary Joseph Ward, Congressman Francis O'Neill and Lt Governor Robert Murphy greet the front-running candidate enthusiastically. As Kennedy prevailed in primary after primary, Democrats increasingly swung behind his campaign, keen to be associated with a winner.

Opposite below: Jack keeps the voters and cameramen happy at International Airport, Los Angeles. As he criss-crossed the country he mastered the art of delivering short, punchy speeches on a range of subjects. His speed-reading, combined with the ability to memorize huge amounts of data, helped him enormously during campaigning.

Jack and Jackie, pictured at Idlewild Airport, New York. Jackie remained at Hyannis Port instead of attending the Democratic Convention which opened on 11 July in Los Angeles. Despite the uncertainties surrounding the nomination, Jack found time to carry on his affair with Judith Campbell.

The ruthless campaign manager

34-year-old Bobby Kennedy was the *éminence grise* behind the scenes. He was ruthlessly efficient, determined to do whatever it took to get his brother elected. As a taskmaster he was as hard on himself as he was on others. He didn't just remain at the nerve center of the campaign, but took on a grueling schedule of meetings in the Midwest, often in atrocious weather conditions.

Kennedy fails to win over former first lady

Above: There is a palpably frosty air as Eleanor Roosevelt exchanges words with Kennedy at the Democratic Convention. The former First Lady was unimpressed by Jack's liberal credentials, and would have supported Adlai Stevenson if the twice-defeated candidate had chosen to run.

Opposite: Kennedy with Frank Sinatra at a fund-raiser on the eve of his selection as the Democratic presidential candidate. Kennedy loved the Hollywood glitz that the entertainer and his coterie represented. It was Sinatra who introduced Jack to Judith Campbell, a mistress he shared with mobster Sam Giancana. 'High Hopes'. Sinatra's famous song became an apposite campaign anthem. However, he would come to be regarded as a liability, and the Kennedys eventually severed all relations with the crooner.

Smiles hide animosity between Kennedy and Johnson

Above: Lyndon Johnson applauds as Kennedy steps up to speak to the Texas Delegation during the Democratic convention. Notwithstanding his success in the primaries, Jack still had to secure the endorsement of his party. Johnson played a waiting game. The Senate Leader hadn't entered the primaries, but felt he could still win the nomination. Exchanges between the two camps in the run-up to the declarations were vitriolic. Kennedy prevailed on the first ballot, with 808 votes to Johnson's 409. Despite the animosity between the two men, Kennedy asked Johnson to be his running mate. The invitation was given - and accepted - for political purposes.

Left: Bobby takes soundings on the floor of the Convention hall. He is pictured talking to his brother-in-law, actor Peter Lawford, who married Patricia Kennedy in 1954. Lawford was a conduit for Jack's extra-curricular activities, organizing parties and providing a steady supply of girls.

Kennedy disappoints black leaders on civil rights

Wisconsin delegate Val Phillips questions the candidate about his commitment to civil rights. Kennedy frustrated black leaders with his refusal to give a firm policy pledge on the issue. This returned to haunt him during his administration, and it would not be until after his death that legislation was finally enacted.

"Little Brother Is Watching You..."

Left: All the Kennedy family worked tirelessly for Jack's election, but it was Bobby who was the lynchpin. He kept campaign workers on their toes, and one coined the expression "Little brother is watching you", indicating that his methods included intimidation as well as exhortation.

Opposite: Jackie was carefully primed during the campaign. She was warned about being drawn on any issue in public, and even smoking was forbidden. Her impact was significant, however. She was the epitome of glamor and style, and countless column inches were devoted to her appearance.

Below: In Jackie's absence, Rose Kennedy occupies the seat next to her son and his running mate at the Democratic Convention. Rose articulated her son's credentials by commenting that he "was rocked to political lullabies".

Opposite below: Bobby Kennedy Jr explains the mysteries of flight to his Uncle Jack as family members return to Boston following the party Convention.

Above: With the nomination secured, Bobby and Ethel Kennedy, along with their children, accompany Jack back to Massachusetts. Bobby had married Ethel Skakel in 1950. He named his first two children Joseph and Kathleen, after the brother and sister he lost.

Opposite above: Missouri senator Stuart Symington was one of the contenders for the Democratic presidential nomination, numbering former president Harry Truman among his supporters. He lacked charisma, however, and came third in the ballot, a long way behind both Kennedy and Johnson. Here he congratulates the worthy victor by holding aloft a copy of the *Detroit Times*.

Jackie welcomes home the candidate

Opposite and Left: Having spent the week of the Convention in an almost deserted Kennedy compound, Jackie welcomes Jack back to Hyannis Port amid tumultuous scenes. In his absence she worked on a painting depicting Jack as Napoleon, with "Il Senatore" inscribed on a three-cornered hat. She presented it to him as a gift to celebrate winning the presidential nomination.

Below: The Kennedys enjoy a day's sailing before the campaign proper gets under way. At this point Jack trailed Republican candidate Richard Nixon in the opinion polls.

Brothers in arms

28-year-old Teddy Kennedy was assigned thirteen western states during the campaign. His penchant for daredevil stunts had more impact than his oratory, as Nixon fared much better than Kennedy in this territory. Bobby was a much more potent figure in the election, a singleminded political fixer who proved to be the ideal person to head up the backroom team.

Bobby demands unity in New York

Opposite above: Feuding Democrats in New York brings Bobby to the city on a peace mission. Here, he discusses the possibility of a temporary truce with Mayor Robert Wagner on the steps of his official residence, Gracie Mansion. Jack knew he had to have a broad appeal if he was to win. He targeted young voters and factory workers in the industrial heartlands of the Northeast. With Johnson on the ticket, the Democrats hoped for a strong showing in the South. In particular it was vital to win back Texas and Louisiana, and hold the Carolinas.

Opposite below: 7 August 1960. Jack and Jackie on board their sailing boat *Wianno Senior*. Jack returned to Washington the following day, and began the task of eating into the Republican lead in the polls.

Above: Jack and Bobby confer prior to a controversial Senate vote on medical care for the elderly. The issue remained unresolved when Congress was adjourned a week later, 1 September 1960.

Journalists ignore Kennedy's womanizing

Left: Jackie embraces her husband in a touching, unposed moment captured through a car window. Jack's infidelity was common knowledge in Washington, but journalists were not interested in the candidate's private peccadilloes.

Opposite: Jackie, pictured at the couple's Georgetown home. She put her creative talents to work in refurbishing their first permanent home, angering her notoriously parsimonious husband.

Below: An off-duty family photograph taken at Cape Cod, just before Jack hit the campaign trail.

Youth and dynamism garner votes

Image played a vital part in the 1960 election campaign. In these terms the Kennedys compared favorably with the outgoing President and First Lady, Dwight and Mamie Eisenhower, and the Nixons. Jack was only four years younger than his Republican rival, but the image gap was much wider. He would be the first White House incumbent to be born in the twentieth century.

Opposite: Jackie and Caroline share a happy moment during a trip to Washington. Despite her wish to support Jack's campaign, Jackie hated the intrusion and loss of privacy that it inevitably brought. Shortly after he won the nomination, she ordered extra fencing to be erected at the "Kennedy Compound" in Hyannis Port, hoping to deter the hordes of sightseers.

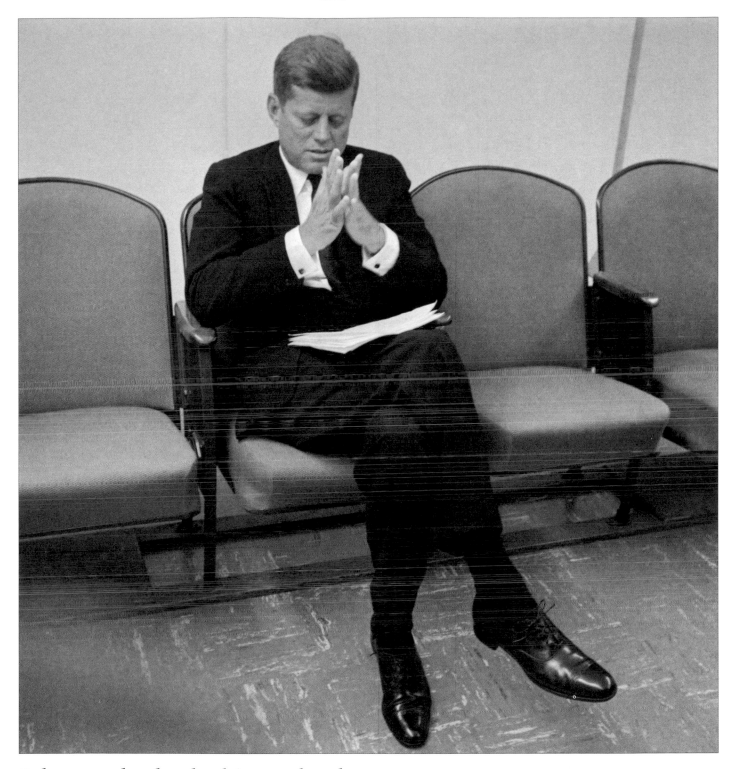

Johnson checks the history books

Opposite above: Bobby Kennedy and Lyndon Johnson show a united front - in public, at least. Privately, Bobby was left fuming at the choice of Johnson as running mate. The Senate majority leader had little time for Bobby, whom he considered a young upstart. Johnson is said to have looked up how many presidents had died in office before agreeing to run for vice-president.

Left: Johnson had more luck with Kennedy females than males when it came to getting them to pose in typical Texas headgear. Ethel Kennedy (left) and Eunice were happy to don cowboy hats for the cameras. Johnson's wife, Lady Bird, pictured second left, had great reservations about her husband agreeing to run as vice-president.

Above: Jack goes over his notes before giving yet another address. The combination of his oratorical skills and Ted Sorensen's speech-writing was a powerful campaigning weapon.

Moving Ahead

Left: 3 September 1960. A two-hour stop in San Francisco en route to Anchorage is more than enough time to deliver another barnstorming speech. He spoke of the New Frontier and Moving Ahead, which would be recurring campaign themes.

Above: All the Kennedy family were mobilized during the campaign. Here, Jack stops off to see his sister, Patricia Lawford, who had three children under five at the time of the election.

Opposite: A moment of quiet reflection during two months of intense politicking. Kennedy toured the country at breakneck speed, visiting far more cities than his Republican opponent.

Kennedy turns Catholic issue to his advantage

Opposite above and below: The Kennedys attend a $100-a-plate fund-raiser in Washington to boost party coffers. Jack made his first nationwide television address at the function. The issue of his Catholicism was much to the fore at this point. Far from being a potential vote-loser, the issue became a positive boon to the Kennedy campaign. In the end it was Nixon who wanted to bury the religious question, while Jack was happy to keep it alive.

Above: As Jackie was in the latter stages of pregnancy, she was unable to keep up with her husband's exhausting schedule. A reception at the Hotel Commodore, New York in mid-September was one of the few times they were able to appear together.

Head to head with Nixon

Below: Kennedy and Nixon observe the social niceties before the first of their four televised debates.

Nixon believed he would get the better of Kennedy in these exchanges. In terms of point-scoring the debates were largely inconclusive. However, while Nixon looked nervous and ill-at-ease, Jack's good looks and charisma made a favorable impression on the voters.

The debates were more noteworthy for the perceptions they created than the merit of the candidates' arguments. The minority who listened on radio thought that Nixon had the edge. But there were now more than 40 million television sets in America, and the vast majority saw a Republican candidate who looked nervous and unhealthy. After the first encounter, Jack was mobbed like a movie star, while Nixon's own mother telephoned to ask if her son was unwell.

Rapturous New York welcome for Kennedys

Below: With three weeks still to go before the election, the Kennedys enjoy a ticker-tape reception in Manhattan. This was Jackie's last campaign appearance with her husband.

Opposite: Jackie holds a press conference at her Washington home. Public speaking was not her forte, and she could be abrasive in such situations.

Left: Kennedy females were brought up to be as competitive and goal-orientated as their brothers. Patricia, Jean and Eunice take a brief break from campaigning to catch up on family matters.

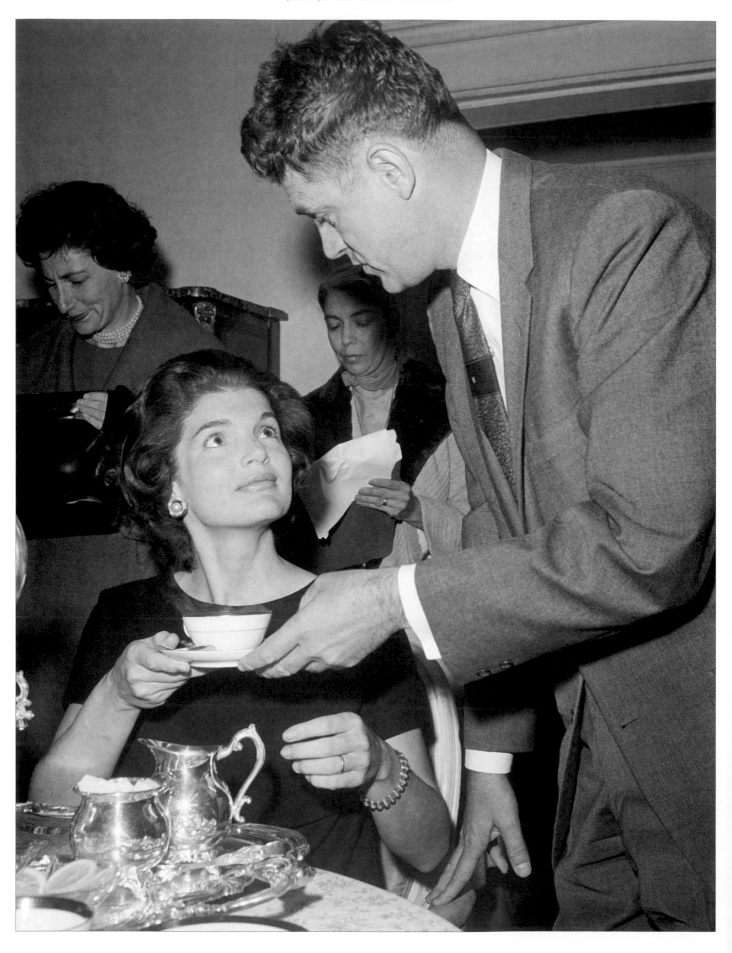

Jackie tackles welfare issues

Above: Jackie meets Katherine Ellickson of the Women's Committee for New Frontier. This was one of several meetings with officials whose expertise was in social policy, and was no doubt used to help counter the view that Jackie, with her cultured ways and expensive tastes, lacked the common touch.

Opposite: Jackie hosted a number of parties at the Kennedys' Washington home. Here, she pours a cup for Democrat John Foley.

The President-elect and the family man

Above: Jack enjoys a brief respite from his grueling schedule to spend some time with Jackie and Caroline. Jack found it easy to reconcile his role as husband and father with his need for casual sex. He was capable of great tenderness and affection where his family was concerned, yet within minutes of being separated from them he could be cavorting with another woman. He saw this as a compartmentalized need rather than a betrayal.

Right: Jackie and Claudia "Lady Bird" Johnson. It was all smiles for the camera, but Lady Bird wept when she learned that her husband had agreed to run as vice-president. The two women were not close, but did share an unwavering support for their husbands' careers. Lady Bird was an experienced political wife and carried off the role with aplomb. When Jackie's pregnancy curtailed her ability to campaign, Lady Bird stepped up her own commitments to compensate.

Above: Jack's heavy campaigning schedule meant that he was an absent father for long periods. It is said that "airplane" was among the first words Caroline Kennedy uttered.

Things were now going well for the Democrats. The TV debates had turned the deficit into a three-point lead for Kennedy. Nixon also blundered when Martin Luther King was jailed during a protest in Atlanta. While he vacillated, Kennedy acted, expediting King's release. This was a turning point in securing the crucial black vote, although when America went to the polls on 8 November, the result was still too close to call.

Closest election ever

Opposite below: Bobby and members of the backroom team study the early election returns. The outcome hung in the balance until 6:00 a.m. on 9 November, when the Michigan result gave Jack the required number of electoral votes for victory.

Right: Jackie, pictured with her mother, Janet Auchinloss. Jackie and her sister went to live with their mother after her marriage to "Black Jack" Bouvier ended. Their relationship was a difficult one; Jackie had more affection for her roguish father.

Below: With just 24 hours to go before polling, Jack prepares to make a final network TV broadcast. New Hampshire is the venue, and Gov. Luther Hodges hosts the proceedings. Eunice, Jean and Pat are on hand to offer their support, while Bobby gives his final words of advice over the phone. After the election, Kennedy would appoint 62-year-old Hodges as Secretary for Commerce, making him the oldest man in the new administration.

Opposite above: Bobby and Ethel Kennedy cast their votes at Hyannis. Jack's electoral address was in Boston, and he voted there before joining the rest of the family.

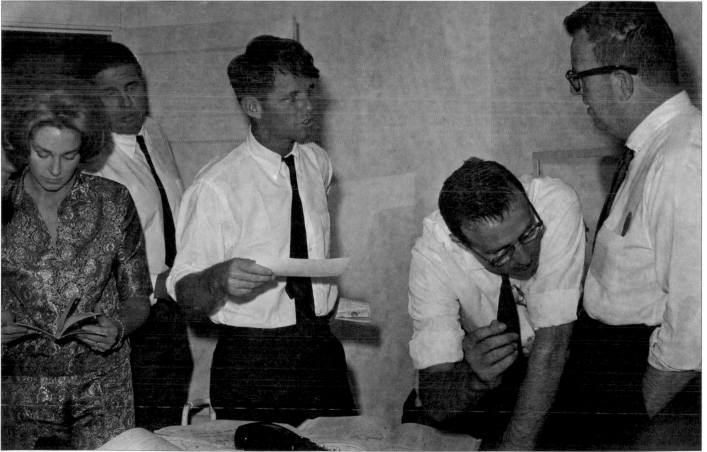

Kennedys out in force to celebrate victory

Above: Eunice, Patricia and Ethel show a mixture of happiness and relief as the tide of the election results starts to turn in Jack's favor.

Opposite above: The Kennedy clan come out in force as Jack makes his victory speech at Hyannis Port Armory on 9 November.

Opposite below: Unlike the rest of the family, Joe had been deliberately kept out of the limelight during the campaign. There had been concern that the Republicans would make political capital out of the suggestion that Jack was merely his father's puppet.

President elect

Opposite: The President-elect and First Lady pose with Joe and Rose Kennedy at Hyannis Port. Jackie got on well with her father-in-law, perhaps seeing shades of her own father in him. Her relationship with Rose was much more strained.

Above: It was not until 5.45 am on 9 November that victory in Michigan gave Kennedy 285 electoral votes, assuring him of victory. The popular vote became the subject of much debate. The official return gave Kennedy 34,227,096 votes to Nixon's 34,108,546. Such a narrow margin, together with rumors of ballot-rigging, prompted Nixon's aides to demand a recount in some of the states where the result had been closest. Nixon refused. He didn't want to be labeled an ungracious loser, something which might have affected his chances in any future bid to reach the White House.

The moment of victory

Hyannis Port, 10 November 1960. After an exhaustive concerted effort, the Kennedy clan are able to relax and savor the moment of victory. Standing (left to right): Ethel Kennedy, Stephen Smith, Jean Kennedy Smith, the President-elect, Bobby Kennedy, Patricia Kennedy Lawford, Sargent Shriver, Joan Kennedy, Peter Lawford. Seated (left to right): Eunice Kennedy, Rose Kennedy, Joseph Kennedy, Jackie and Teddy Kennedy.

Fatherhood second time round

Left: Jack was on board *Caroline* bound for Florida when he received word that Jackie had gone into labor and been rushed into hospital. John F. Kennedy Jr was born by Cesarean section before Jack could return to Washington.

Opposite: Jack arrives at Georgetown Hospital, Washington, to visit Jackie and his newborn son. He played the doting father to the full, and his behavior was in marked contrast to the callous way he acted when Jackie lost a child in 1956.

Below: Kennedy and Nixon shake hands for the cameras as they meet in Florida a week after the election. Even though he chose not to challenge the result, Nixon was undoubtedly aggrieved. He arranged to have his speech conceding defeat read for him, prompting Jack to remark: "He went out the way he came in - no class."

Bobby to head up Justice Department

Opposite: The President names the new Attorney General on the front steps of his Georgetown home. Both men had great reservations about putting Bobby in charge of the Justice Department. The fact that he had no legal training would inevitably bring forth accusations of nepotism. Jack told Bobby not to smile; he didn't want to give the appearance that they were overly happy about the appointment. Ironically, while Bobby accepted the Attorney Generalship, it was his younger brother, Teddy, who was the law student. It wouldn't be long before the family would turn its efforts towards helping Teddy forge a political career in his own right.

Above: John F. Kennedy Jr is shown off to the press after his christening at the Georgetown University hospital chapel. The baby had been born a month premature. He suffered from a serious lung condition and it was thought he might not survive. Jackie's health was also in a parlous state. After the birth, both her physical and mental well-being gave great cause for concern.

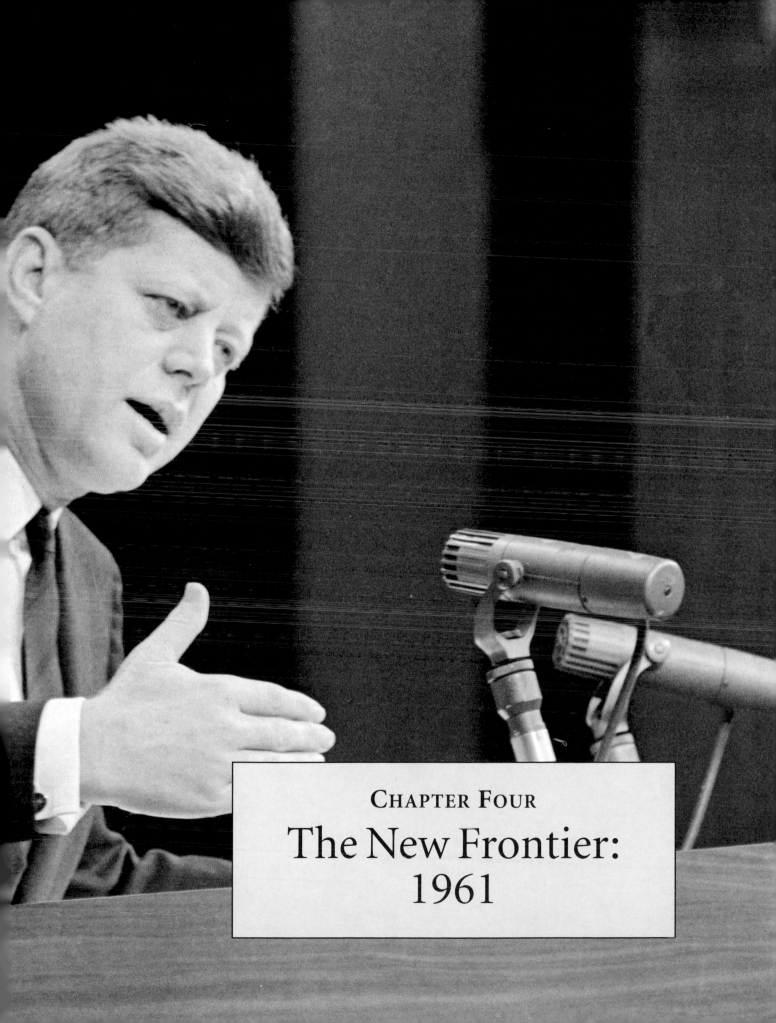

CHAPTER FOUR
The New Frontier:
1961

J FK's inauguration took place on 20 January 1961. It was a bright but bitterly cold day, yet Jack, true to the image of robust vitality he had fostered, braved the ceremony without hat or coat. Also typically, the outward appearance didn't tell the whole story, for Jack took the precaution of wearing thermal underwear.

Jack wanted the proceedings to be imbued with cultural as well as political significance. Robert Frost, eighty-six years old and one of the country's most distinguished men of letters, was invited to read a piece composed specially for the occasion. Its theme was hope and optimism, with the country about to enter a golden age of poetry and power. The blinding light meant that Frost was unable to complete the piece, which was to be a preface to an earlier work. He recited that poem from memory instead. It contained the line "Such as we were we gave ourselves outright", which was supremely apposite for the occasion.

At 12.51 Chief Justice Earl Warren administered the oath, and JFK was sworn in to preside over an administration that was to last 1037 days.

The inaugural address was a masterpiece of rhetoric and delivery. It had gone through countless drafts over many weeks. Jack was the overseer, honing and tweaking, but as ever the mastermind was Sorensen. It paid due respect to the country's heritage and proud traditions, but its central theme was moving forward. The future would bring many challenges, "the common enemies of man: tyranny, poverty, disease and war itself". The struggle against these evils and the defense of freedoms America held so dear would come at a price, however, and sacrifice would be needed. "And so, my fellow Americans, ask not what your country can do for you - ask what you can do for your country." The emphasis on global rather than domestic issues was deliberate, and presaged the amount of time and energy the new president would devote to foreign affairs.

Kennedy had referred to "a new generation of Americans" in his address, and his program was called the New Frontier. However, his first executive decisions were firmly rooted in the past. He reappointed J. Edgar Hoover and Allen Dulles as head of the FBI and CIA respectively, to the dismay of many of his supporters. Kennedy liked to surround himself with liberal intellectuals, such as J. K. Galbraith, but when it came to making appointments he valued those who could act as well as think. Hoover and Dulles were almost national institutions at the time; besides, they were in possession of much sensitive information, such as Jack's adulterous behavior and the unvarnished truth about his wartime exploits. It made sense to have them on board.

Dean Rusk, a Rhodes scholar and head of the Rockefeller Foundation, was appointed Secretary of State. Robert McNamara was given the defense portfolio. McNamara had recently been appointed head of the Ford Motor Company. A Phi Beta Kappa graduate of the University of California, he was a deep thinker as well as an outstanding businessman. For the sensitive Treasury job Jack again played safe and decided on C. Douglas Dillon, the under-

Left: Leaving for the Inaugural Gala, 20 January 1961. Jackie's white satin gown was designed by Oleg Cassini.

secretary in the outgoing administration. Jack was more interested in surrounding himself with high achievers than - in McNamara's and Dillon's case - their Republican leanings. Indeed, most of his appointments were conservative, and they embraced bi-partisanship. They did little for the civil rights movement, however; no black was given any senior post in the administration.

The most controversial decision was handing the attorney generalship to thirty-four-year-old Bobby. To install someone who hadn't studied law as head of the Justice Department, with its 30,000-strong staff, was bound to invite charges of nepotism. Bobby himself had been reluctant to accept at first, relenting only after Jack reiterated his need to have someone absolutely trustworthy in that key position. Another Kennedy prominent in Jack's administration,

though without a portfolio, was his father. Joe had melted into the background during the campaign as a hedge against allegations that a vote for Jack was a vote for the elder Kennedy. Now it was perfectly safe for Joe to return to the stage, and since the election the two had been in regular contact.

Kennedy's men were the brightest and best. Even so, Jack by instinct and inclination was no committee man or easy delegator. He intended to assume the role of chief executive in the fullest sense of the word. He was also much more concerned with tackling immediate issues than long-term strategic planning. It wouldn't be long before he got the opportunity to make some decisions of global significance.

Kennedy's first State of the Union address, on 30 January 1961, was solemn in tone. The dangers

Left: The President-elect at the Miami Orange Bowl, 2 January 1961.
Above: January 1961. The first family returns to Washington.

posed by the Cold War were highlighted by the fact that Communism had established a foothold just ninety miles from American soil, in Fidel Castro's Cuba. Jack was acutely aware that Cuba was one of several potential flashpoints where there was a potential for conflict between East and West. Nikita Khrushchev, while congratulating Kennedy on his election victory, also made it clear that the Soviet Union stood four-square behind any insurgents who sought to liberate their country from capitalist imperialists. Communism would spread through a succession of wars of liberation in the Third World. Jack, a firm believer in the Domino Theory, took this threat very seriously. He had two responses to it; the

first was open and diplomatic, the second covert and militaristic.

The diplomatic initiatives were the Peace Corps and the Alliance For Progress. The former, which was established on 1 March, involved sending teams of highly skilled volunteers to developing countries to help them tackle economic and social problems. The latter was aimed specifically at Latin American countries, helping them to improve standards in health and education, and achieve economic stability. Both initiatives had noble aims, but the secondary objective was not hard to discern: the administration wanted to attack the conditions which could all too easily create revolutionary zealots.

If diplomatic initiatives failed to secure stable, anti-Communist buffer zones, there remained the military option. And as far as Cuba was concerned, it was already too late for diplomacy. Jack had inherited a CIA operation in which anti-Castro Cuban exiles were being trained and equipped in Guatemala. The objective of Operation Pluto was for this 1500-strong force to ignite a widespread uprising on the island, and topple its Marxist government. Running in tandem was a separate plot in which the help of Mafia bosses was enlisted for an assassination attempt on the Cuban leader. Eisenhower may not have known about the involvement of mobsters; given that Sam Giancana was one of those consulted, it is barely conceivable that Kennedy didn't know, and approve, of this course of action. In the event, two attempts were made on Castro's life before the invasion took place.

On 15 April, following a preliminary airstrike by six B-26 bombers, Kennedy gave the green light for the invasion to go ahead. Against the wishes of military chiefs, it was decided that the Bay of Pigs would be the landing site. It was swampy terrain, a hundred miles west of Trinidad. Castro was already on full alert. The planned invasion was virtually common knowledge; only the time and place remained unknown. The airstrike made no serious dent in Castro's arsenal, but it did remove the element of surprise. When the invading force landed in the early hours of Monday 17 April, the whole plan quickly unraveled. Jack was in a quandary; he was naturally drawn to the idea of an audacious raid, but he was desperate to preserve the fiction that the exiles were acting alone. He wasn't helped by the fact that both hawks and doves were vying for his ear. CIA Deputy Director Richard Bissell, the plan's architect, emphasized the importance of decisive, prompt action. Dean Rusk and Arthur Schlesinger Jr were among those who thought the enterprise flawed.

Jack canceled a second airstrike, which was to have provided cover while the invading force established a beachhead. Cuban aircraft thus met with no resistance as they sank two supply ships. The invaders were quickly overwhelmed, with 114 killed and 1189 captured. Jack was devastated at the news of such an ignominious defeat.

He made a brave fist of it. In the wake of the debacle he remained combative, committed to the fight against Communism on America's doorstep. He also assumed total responsibility for the enterprise, something which helped to preserve his popularity. Privately he was seething, feeling he had been misled into thinking it was a high-reward, low-risk operation.

Protracted negotiations began to free the captives. A deal was eventually struck for their release, the USA paying some $56 million in cash and goods. It was condemned by some as a squalid form of bartering, tantamount to the USA yielding to blackmail. But with the threat of trial and execution hanging over the captives' heads, many heaped praise on Kennedy for his statesmanlike behavior and compassion. On 29 December a rally was held at Miami's Orange Bowl to celebrate the captives' release. Jack was in upbeat mood, stressing that the Bay of Pigs represented only a temporary reversal. By then a new plan was in place, Operation Mongoose. The aim remained the same, but this time it would be achieved by stealth and infiltration. Propaganda and sabotage would be the main weapons in destabilizing the Castro regime and ultimately removing its leader.

Two more theaters of potential East-West conflict provided Kennedy with much food for thought in the early days of his presidency: Southeast Asia and Berlin. Since the defeat of the French at Dien Bien Phu in 1954, America had strongly supported South Vietnam's non-Communist regime, headed by Ngo Dinh Diem. By mid-1961, Diem's government was very unpopular and looked a prime target for forces from the Communist North. Kennedy sent Johnson to Saigon to assess the situation, and the vice-president reported back suggesting a major US deployment in the area. Kennedy balked at the idea. With the Bay of Pigs fiasco fresh in memory - and that with Cuba just ninety miles away - he was circumspect about fighting a war thousands of miles from home. He opted instead for a huge increase in aid to help prop up Diem's ailing regime.

Left: September 1961. The President and First Lady attend Mass at St Francis Xavier, Hyannis, where many of the Kennedy family services were held.

An even more immediate problem was Laos. Pathet Lao guerrilla forces, with backing from Hanoi and Moscow, were making inroads in a country that Kennedy, like Eisenhower before him, regarded as a strategic bulwark against Communism. By the time Kennedy came face to face with Khrushchev in Vienna, in June 1961, there was an uneasy cease-fire in Laos. The two leaders reaffirmed their desire to end hostilities in the country, although this would prove to be a temporary respite.

In late May 1961 the Kennedys embarked on a state visit to Europe. For Jackie the first six months of the presidency had revolved around organizing the refurbishment of the White House. Her grandiose plans to replace poor reproductions with period pieces quickly consumed the government funds allocated, and became another source of friction between her and her notoriously parsimonious husband. Clothes were another passion for the First Lady. She had appointed Oleg Cassini as her official designer, and he had been the inspiration behind the woolen coat and pillbox hat worn by Jackie at the Inauguration and much copied thereafter.

Jackie dazzled during the first leg of the European visit, to France. Jack, noting the impact his chic and beautiful wife had on the crowds, quipped that he was "the man who accompanied Jackie Kennedy to Paris".

JFK's talks with Charles de Gaulle were cordial. The two agreed that any Soviet action which threatened West Berlin's status had to be resisted. Speaking from bitter experience, France's president also cautioned Kennedy about military involvement in Southeast Asia.

The Kennedys moved on to Vienna, where Jack had a torrid time in his two-day summit with Khrushchev. There was agreement that Laos should be neutral, but there were frosty exchanges over West Berlin. Kennedy reiterated that the US would go to any lengths to defend the status quo. Khrushchev talked of signing a treaty with East Germany, a clear threat to NATO forces in the divided city. The potential escalation was made more worrying by the lack of agreement over nuclear testing. Kennedy had been put on the back foot as he headed for Britain and a meeting with Prime Minister Harold Macmillan. He wasn't helped by the fact that he was suffering severe back pain at the time, for which he had begun taking amphetamines. In a volatile situation Kennedy was thus taking substances that were known to impair judgment.

On 13 August there was a new and dramatic turn of events. East Germany, desperate to stem the flow of defections to West Berlin, which was running at thousands per day, began to construct a wall across the city. West Germany looked to Kennedy for an immediate and strong response. He opted for a more measured reaction, ordering a convoy of 1500 troops on a 110-mile journey from West Germany along the autobahn into West Berlin. They arrived unhindered. Ironically, after the initial posturing, the building of the Wall actually eased East-West tensions. Khrushchev didn't sign the treaty with East Germany, and West Berlin remained open.

By now, the "Hundred Days of Action" that Kennedy had spoken of had long since elapsed. He knew all along that this was just electoral posturing, as the prevailing climate in no way resembled that which Roosevelt had inherited. With the exception of the founding of the Peace Corps, the early months accomplished little of substance.

One notable area of presidential inactivity was on the issue of civil rights. The battle to end discrimination should have sat comfortably on the agenda of a Democratic president, and high on it too. During the hustings Jack had spoken of ending segregation in federal housing "at the stroke of the pen". Yet even this small matter remained unaddressed at the end of 1961. The lack of action disappointed liberals who were seeking major reforms and in May 1961, two busloads representing the Congress of Racial Equality decided to take matters into their own hands. Dubbed "Freedom Riders", they drove into Mississippi and Alabama to protest against segregation. There were other ugly scenes, and federal marshals had to be deployed to restore order. Bobby was sent in as peacemaker; he exhorted black leaders to seek redress through the ballot box, rather than demonstrations. He also made representations to the transport industry, calling for an end to segregation in bus, rail and air travel. The black population was less than impressed at such

half-hearted measures, and the civil rights issue would return to haunt the Kennedy administration.

May 5, 1961 did give the country the fillip of putting a man into space, albeit a month after the Russians had done so. Jack saw the prestige of being ahead in the space race, and spoke of America putting a man on the moon before the end of the decade.

Jack's first year in office ended with yet another family tragedy. Seventy-three-year-old Joe suffered a massive stroke, leaving him partially paralyzed and without the power of speech. Joe had orchestrated his son's rise to the White House, and

the two were in regular contact after Jack took office. The president could no longer look to his father for advice and support. On the other hand, he no longer had to worry about living up to Joe's expectations or seeking his approval. And even before his father became incapacitated, Jack had already begun asserting his independence. The discussions between them had become increasingly perfunctory. No one could now accuse Jack of not being his own man.

Head of Ford Motor Co. gets defense portfolio

Opposite above: The president confers with his new Defense Secretary, Robert McNamara. McNamara was a typical "New Frontiersman" in the Kennedy administration. A year older than Jack, he was an intellectual but with a reputation for getting things done. Jack lured him from his post as head of the Ford Motor Co., and was not unduly worried about his Republican leanings.

Opposite below: Kennedy liked to take soundings from liberal intellectuals, such as Harvard professor Arthur Schlesinger Jr, who was appointed as a special adviser. However, he was a pragmatist by instinct, and was more interested in achieving immediate goals than long-term strategic planning.

Above: The President-elect braves the elements as he leaves for yet another function held in his honor. The Inauguration also took place in freezing conditions, yet Jack made a point of appearing hatless and coatless. He liked to present an image of athleticism and vigor, but on that occasion he made sure he was wearing thermal underwear.

Inagaural day

Previous Page: The presidential party is given an enthusiastic reception during the Inaugural Parade. Green dye had been sprayed on the grass to give an appearance of spring rather than winter, and flame-throwers were used to melt the snow which fell in the hours leading up to the ceremony.

With their new home in the background, the Kennedys make their way to the Inaugural Parade. Jackie's wool coat and pillbox hat were by Oleg Cassini, whom she had appointed her personal designer. She demanded exclusivity, making it clear that she didn't want to see any "fat little women" attired in any identical outfit.

The passing of power

Above: The outgoing chief executive Dwight Eisenhower was 70 when he left office, making him the oldest man to occupy the White House. At 43, JFK was the youngest elected president ever. Eisenhower told his successor that the situation in Southeast Asia would give him much cause for concern. Despite their differences, Kennedy subscribed to Eisenhower's view that the countries of Indochina could fall to Communism one by one at an alarming rate, a world view that came to be known as the Domino Theory.

Opposite: The Kennedys leave the Capitol building at the end of the ceremony which saw Jack sworn in as the 35th president of United States. Jackie was extremely ill on the day, and the Kennedys' personal physician Janet Travell prescribed Dexedrine to help her get through the exhausting schedule.

Gala celebrations usher in new administration

Above: Frank Sinatra escorts Jackie to her box for a glittering evening of entertainment at the National Guard Armory on the eve of the Inauguration. Jack gave Sinatra a warm vote of thanks for organizing the fund-raiser. Sinatra saw the tribute as recognition of the part he had played in getting Kennedy elected.

Opposite below: Gala celebrations were held at five different venues to usher in the new administration. Jackie cut her evening short and returned to the White House alone. Jack partied long into the night.

Opposite above: The presidential box at the Inaugural Ball. Joe and Rose Kennedy are seated to the President's right. Jackie is in conversation with Lyndon Johnson and Teddy Kennedy sits behind.

First Bill signed

Opposite below: Congressmen from both Houses present Jack with a pair of cufflinks to mark the signing of his first Bill as chief executive. The new legislation increased the amount of government food surpluses to be distributed to the country's poorest families.

Opposite above: In an early press conference, Kennedy deflects media questions regarding the existence of a "missile gap" between the USA and the Soviet Union. There was indeed a gap, but it was in America's favor. During the election campaign Jack preserved the fiction of superior Soviet arms capability for political purposes.

Above: The Kennedy's return to Washington after a weekend break in Palm Beach. Jack had just made his first State of the Union address, in which he warned of the dangers posed by Communism. Caroline and John Jr had to remain in Palm Beach initially, while Jackie supervised getting their rooms at the White House ready. The press was out in force on 4 February, when Jack and Jackie finally brought the children home. Jackie swaddled John Jr in blankets, trying to shield the baby from his first taste of media intrusion.

Peace Corps founded

Opposite above: Bobby Kennedy's wife, Ethel (left) attends a press conference with Jean and Eunice Kennedy. The theme was the Peace Corps, one of Jack's most popular and successful initiatives. The idea was to send highly skilled volunteers to developing countries, where they would give assistance in any number of areas, from infrastructure projects to social policy matters. The conference was led by Sargent Shriver, Eunice Kennedy's husband, who was charged with implementing the program.

Opposite below: 1 March 1960. Kennedy invites Eleanor Roosevelt to the White House on the day the Peace Corps officially came into being. The President was always keen to exploit the public relations value of any policy announcements.

Above: Caroline Kennedy plays with her two-month-old baby brother, John F. Kennedy Jr.

Sisters meet in Washington

Above: Jackie, pictured with her sister Lee, who was married to Prince Stanislaus Radziwill. When they were growing up, Jackie regarded Lee as the beauty of the family. She believed that her own strengths were intellectectual rather than physical.

Opposite above: The last Democratic president, Harry S. Truman, pays a visit to the Oval Office. Unlike his father, Jack had been a keen supporter of the Truman Doctrine, which gave aid to European countries to help stave off the threat of Communism. It was not a mutual appreciation society, however. Truman had grave reservations about Kennedy's suitability for the role of chief executive.

Opposite below: Kennedy visits Honduras, where he is received by President Ramon Villeda. Jack had talks with leaders of all Central American countries during his visit, apprising them of his Alliance for Progress initiative. Its aim was to help improve the economies and welfare systems of Latin American countries. This was not implemented purely for altruistic reasons. Kennedy knew that grinding poverty and lack of access to decent housing, education and health care would inevitably mean continuing political instability. It was not in the United States' interest to see the rise to power of more revolutionaries like Fidel Castro, the Cuban leader who had overthrown the Batista government in 1959.

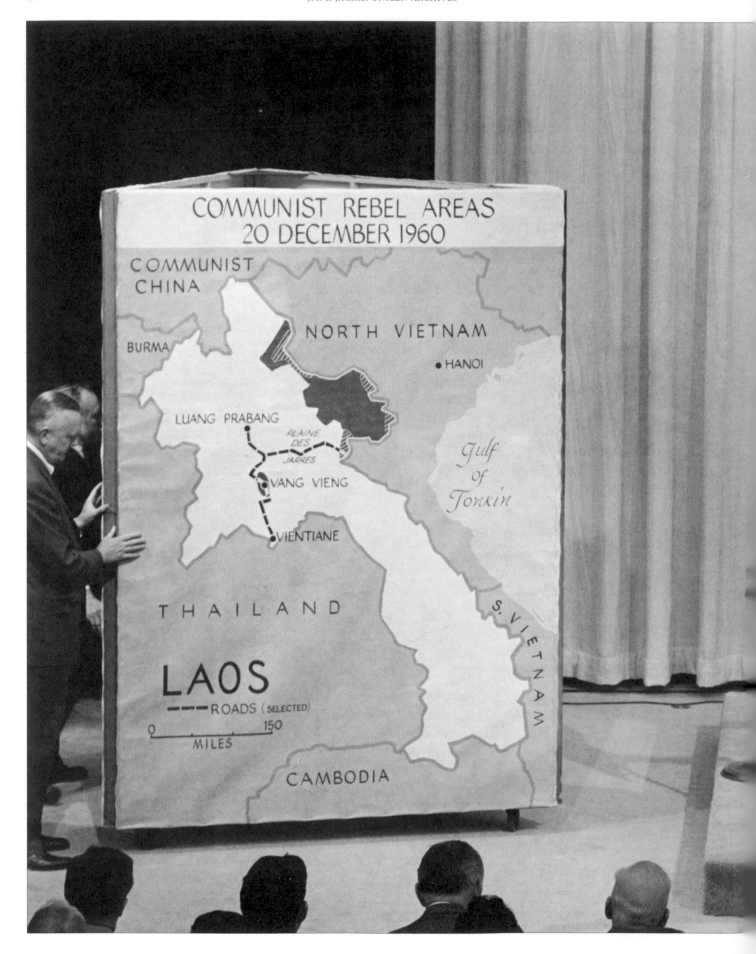

President warns of threat to Laos

March 22, 1961. Kennedy uses a map of Southeast Asia to illustrate the growth of Communism in the region. He highlighted the strategic importance of preventing Laos from becoming the next domino to fall. However, the Bay of Pigs reversal made Jack think twice about a military option, which some of his advisers were already recommending. Instead, Jack favored a continuation of aid in support of those fighting the Communist Pathet Lao, who were being backed by North Vietnam and the Soviet Union. If a pro-Western regime could not take control in Laos, Jack felt that the second-best option was to secure a cease-fire and neutrality for the country. This would be high on the agenda during Kennedy's summit meeting with Khrushchev in June.

First Lady plans grand White House refurbishment scheme

Above: The First Lady, pictured after attending an Easter service at Palm Beach. Almost as soon as she took up residence at the White House, Jackie instituted plans for a grand refurbishment program. She had been dismayed by the contents when her predecessor, Mamie Eisenhower, invited her to take a tour of the mansion. Her plan was to remove all the bad reproductions and restore the White House in a grand style befitting its traditions. Owing to the restricted funds available for the project, she arranged to borrow paintings from the National Gallery and Smithsonian. She also asked around among friends to see if they could contribute suitable trinkets and ornaments.

Opposite: At work in the Oval Office. Kennedy allowed journalists unprecedented access to the center of power. It was an exercise in open government, and was also good for his approval ratings.

In early March, Jackie's sister, Lee, came to stay at the White House with her second husband, Stanislaus Radziwill. Radziwill was a Polish prince who became a successful property developer in Britain after leaving his homeland during the war. Jackie went to great lengths to impress her sister and brother-in-law, treating them more like foreign dignitaries than family. Jackie accompanied the Radziwills to Glen Ora, the Kennedy's newly-acquired country retreat, and they then went on to New York, where Jackie indulged her passion for antiques hunting. Just three months had elapsed since the Kennedys had taken up residence at the White House, yet Jackie was already deliberately spending a considerable amount of time away from Washington. She decided she had little choice but to give Jack the space and freedom to relax with his coterie of male friends. Various parts of the White House were used for holding parties in her absence, from the swimming pool to the President and First Lady's private quarters.

Opposite: Jack and his sister Jean, pictured at a baseball game in April 1961. Team sports continued to play a big part in the family's lives. Jackie had little time for such diversions.

US will forge ahead in space race

Above: Jack pledges to make inroads into the lead the Soviet Union enjoyed in the field of space technology. A month after Yuri Gagarin orbited the earth, Alan Shepard became America's first astronaut. Following Shepard's 15-minute flight which took him 115 miles into space, Kennedy declared that it was America's aim to put a man on the moon before the end of the decade.

Opposite above: A good-humored moment shared by Kennedy and the British Prime Minister Harold Macmillan. The two leaders met for the first time in Washington in early April and got on famously.

Opposite below: Jack and ex-president Eisenhower tour the grounds of Camp David.

Camp David, Maryland. Jack canvasses the opinion of former President Eisenhower, in the wake of the Bay of Pigs debacle. The plan to invade Cuba using a brigade of exiles from the country was hatched by the CIA during the Eisenhower administration. When Jack took office, the head of the CIA, Allen Dulles, and his deputy, Richard Bissell, sought permission to carry the plan through. Jack was circumspect, but gave his guarded approval as there was near unanimous agreement that there would be a successful outcome. It turned into a catalog of error and misjudgment which bordered on the farcical. Publicly, Jack took full responsibility; in private he was livid with the advisers who he felt had misled him. As a distinguished military man, Eisenhower was scathing about the way the operation was handled.

Bay of Pigs invasion

Above: The Kennedys in jovial mood in early May 1961. The ignominious end to the Bay of Pigs invasion just a few days earlier failed to dent his popularity. His approval rating actually soared to 82%, prompting a bewildered Kennedy to remark that the more mistakes he made, the more popular he seemed to become.

Opposite above: Jack enjoying a round of golf at Palm Beach with his father and brothers-in-law Stephen Smith (left) and Peter Lawford.

Opposite below: April 1961. Kennedy receives Indonesia's President Sukarno at Andrews Air Force Base. He quickly concluded that international affairs was the field which mattered most and the one in which he would make his mark as a statesman.

44th birthday celebrations

Left: May 29, 1961. Kennedy is guest of honor at Boston's Commonwealth Armory as he celebrates his 44th birthday. With him is Cardinal Richard Cushing, a long-standing family friend who had officiated at many Kennedy weddings, baptisms and funerals. After Kennedy's assassination, the Cardinal admitted being party to distributing donations to various ministries during the election campaign. The link between moneys paid and votes accrued was clearly established.

Opposite: Commitment to the space race inevitably meant huge financial investment. Jack goes before Congress to ask for between 7 and 9 billion dollars over a five-year period. The request was approved, allowing the Apollo program to get under way.

Above: Jack addressing Congress at the mid-year State of the Union address, 25 May 1961.

On the world stage

Jack and Jackie relax at Palm Beach ahead of a heavy touring schedule. It began with a state visit to Canada on 17 May. This was followed by a trip to Paris and Vienna, where the Kennedys would meet political heavyweights Charles De Gaulle and Nikita Khrushchev. Jackie was still riddled with self-doubt over the role of First Lady, particularly when she had to play hostess to a steady stream of senior diplomats and heads of state. The conflict between her distaste for the role and her desire to discharge her duties took a heavy emotional toll. She suffered from mood swings, headaches and depression. Ironically, however, it was during the visit to Canada and Europe that she grabbed the headlines, beguiled some of the world's foremost statesmen and established herself as a star performer on the international stage.

The toast of Paris

Opposite below: Jackie's glamor and style, together with her appreciation of the French language and culture wins over the Parisian crowds. She is depicted leaving the museum of Jeu de Paume, famous for its Impressionist paintings.

Above: Leaving the Elysée Palace, where the Kennedys had dined with President De Gaulle. Both made a favorable impression on the French leader, although he thought the president's youth was a handicap. After the bitter experience the French had had in Indochina, he warned Kennedy of the dangers of becoming embroiled in a conflict in that region.

Opposite above: Jackie chats to journalists at the American Embassy before attending a state banquet at the Palace of Versailles. She wore a Givenchy gown for the occasion, endearing her still further to the French public.

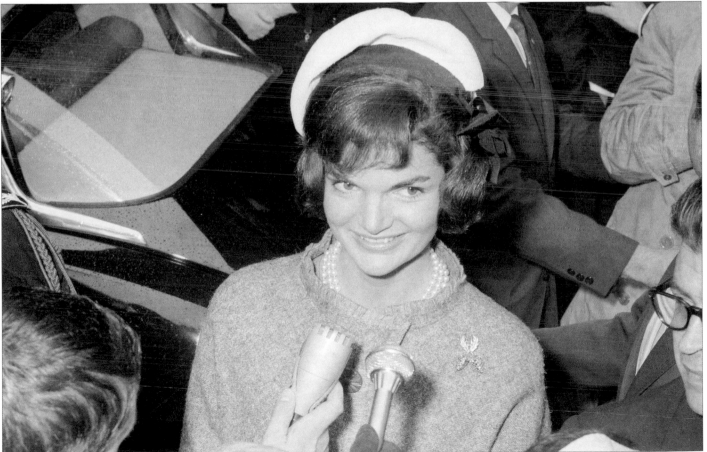

Advantage Khruschev in summit battle

Opposite below: Vienna, June 3, 1961. The official photo-call between the leaders of the East and West suggested a cordial relationship. In fact, Kennedy came away from the two-day summit somewhat shell-shocked. Khrushchev was militaristic, threatening to sign a treaty with East Germany which would put the security of West Berlin at risk.

Opposite above: Kennedy, pictured with some of his top aides. They were summoned to France to prepare the strategic line Jack would take in the summit with Soviet leader Nikita Khrushchev. The guidance and advice received could hardly have prepared him for the encounter. Khrushchev easily got the better of him when the two engaged in a debate on political philosophy. At every turn of the discussion Kennedy found the Soviet leader aggressive and intransigent. When the summit was over, Jack likened negotiating with Khrushchev to dealing with his father: in both cases it was he who was expected to defer.

Above: Kennedy reaffirms US commitment to the defense of Europe in a speech at the Supreme Headquarters of the Allied Powers, Rocquencourt, France.

President and First Lady at Buckingham Palace

Above: The Kennedys ended their state visit to Europe in London. After attending the christening of Prince and Princess Radziwill's daughter Christina, the President and First Lady were guests of honor at a banquet hosted by Queen Elizabeth II at Buckingham Palace. It was the first time an American president had dined at the Palace since 1918, when Woodrow Wilson visited King George V.

Opposite below: Leaving the Radziwills' for the Palace. For Jack, the most important part of this final leg of the trip was to seek Macmillan's advice on his uncomfortable experience of the Vienna summit.

Opposite above: Khrushchev was much more taken with the First Lady than with the President. After outmaneuvering Kennedy during their first meeting, the Soviet leader repeated the trick at the evening's state dinner, held at Schonbrunn Palace. Reporters wanted the leaders to shake hands; Khruschev joked that he preferred to shake Jackie's hand first.

Jackie and her sister shopping in Bond Street, the heart of London's famous jewelry quarter. During their London trip, the Kennedys stayed at the Radziwills' home in Buckingham Place. Queen Elizabeth broke with protocol and invited Lee and Stanislaus Radziwill to the official banquet. Both had been divorced, which was normally a bar to such royal invitations.

The pressures of office

25 July 1961: Jack mops his brow during an address to the nation over the Berlin crisis. After the Bay of Pigs failure, Jack was keen to send out a signal that the freedom of West Berlin would be preserved, by force if necessary.

The war on crime

Above: September 13, 1961. The president signs the Crime Bill, with both the Attorney General, Robert Kennedy, and FBI Director J. Edgar Hoover (second left) in attendance. Mafia bosses were said to be angry at the administration's war against organized crime. They regarded this as a betrayal of the pre-election understanding which had seen them working behind the scenes for a Democratic victory.

Opposite: After a successful six-month trial period, the Peace Corps becomes enshrined in law. Kennedy shakes hands with his brother-in-law Sargent Shriver, the organization's first director.

Action man - with a little help from Dr Feel Good

Above: Jack arriving at Andrews Air Force Base en route to Hyannis Port, early November 1961. The picture suggests vitality, but Jack had been suffering considerable back pain in recent months and had been taking a cocktail of drugs to ease the condition. The man who administered them was Max Jacobson, a New York physician with a cult following who was known as Dr Feel Good. Jackie also received regular injections from Jacobson.

Opposite above: Jack temporarily puts aside the affairs of state to enjoy at a cigar at a Washington banquet in late September 1961. Privately he was highly critical of his own performance during his first nine months in office.

Opposite below: Harry Truman and his wife Bess are guests of honor at a White House dinner, held on 1 November 1961. Truman supported the strong stance Kennedy took after the erection of the Berlin Wall in August that year.

Dulles resigns

Opposite above: Former head of the CIA Allen Dulles receives a National Security Award from the president. Dulles resigned in the wake of the Bay of Pigs fiasco. Jack took the flak in public, but in private he was scathing about the contribution of some of his senior advisers, including Dulles.

Opposite below: 25 November 1961. Jack discusses US nuclear policy with Aleksei Adzhubei, the editor of *Izvestia* and also Nikita Khrushchev's son-in-law. It was the first time the Soviet Union's official newspaper had carried an interview with an American president.

Above: December 1961. Jackie dazzles the Venezuelan public with a speech in La Morita, delivered in perfect Spanish. Looking on is the country's president, Romulo Betancourt. He and Colombia's Alberto Camargo were two of Latin America's most progressive leaders, and Jack deliberately chose these two countries for his first presidential visit to this region. In supporting these regimes, Jack believed it would be more difficult for Communism to make significant inroads.

Opposite: Jackie's first official photograph as the wife of the president. This portrait, by New York photographer Mark Shaw, was used to satisfy the huge number of requests for a picture of the First Lady.

Above: Jack and Jackie attend church service at Palm Beach, 24 December 1961. The seasonal family celebrations were overshadowed by the severe stroke which Joe Kennedy suffered on 19 December.

CHAPTER FIVE
Crisis and Separation: 1962

The new year brought a host of new crises, domestic, foreign and personal. It started well enough. On 20 February, John Glenn became the first American to orbit the earth, vindicating the vocal and financial support Kennedy had pledged to the space program. This achievement came hard on the heels of a political coup, the release of Gary Powers. Powers had been held in Russia on spying charges since May 1960, when his U-2 plane had been shot down. The quid pro quo for Powers' release had been freeing Colonel Rudolph Abel, who was himself serving a thirty-year jail sentence as a Russian spy.

Jack had barely time to bask in the glory of these achievements when he found himself embroiled in a confrontation with the steel industry. He was furious when some of the country's top bosses raised their prices when he had specifically called for restraint from both sides of industry. Fearing the loss of lucrative government contracts and legal action under antitrust laws, the will of the steel men slowly crumbled. Kennedy also made it clear that they risked having any dirt in their private lives exposed. With a combination of carrot and stick, he got his way.

Predictably, Republicans were incandescent, regarding the president's intervention as an unwarranted attack on the free enterprise culture which was central to the country's values. Jack saw the need to redress the balance. Having made his point, during the remainder of his tenure he instituted a string of measures which helped big business, and in summer 1962 he agreed to a $10 billion tax cut which went into the pockets of the country's wealthiest people.

Meanwhile, the cracks continued to show in the Kennedys' marriage. Jack didn't let the affairs of state get in the way of his womanizing. There were many casual conquests, and he initiated a more intense liaison with Mary Meyer, a woman he knew from his college days. Meyer, Judith Campbell and any number of others represented a potential threat to the presidency, but at least they were relatively anonymous figures. The same could hardly be said of Marilyn Monroe. Exactly when Jack first met the screen legend is unclear, but the reverberations of their relationship would soon be echoing through the White House. Jack's weakness for beautiful women and Hollywood glitz, together with Monroe's drink and drug-fueled instability would prove to be a dangerous cocktail.

To mark the refurbishment of the presidential home, Jackie hosted a network television program in which she described the renovations and acquisitions that had been made. Jack had been apprehensive as to how the alterations would play with the public. He needn't have worried, as the program was greeted with enthusiasm. The following month, Jackie embarked on a solo three-week trip to India and Pakistan. She charmed the respective heads of state, Nehru and Ayub, no mean diplomatic feat given the political sensitivies in that part of the world. Jackie would take many more single trips thereafter, physical separation reflecting the emotional distance between them.

The Kennedys spent Easter at Palm Beach, where Joe was preparing for a lengthy rehabilitation program. Jack returned to Washington at the end of April for talks with Macmillan. Britain's premier was not being accompanied by his wife, Lady Dorothy, so Jackie stayed on at Palm Beach. The two leaders met just as the United

States resumed atmospheric nuclear tests at Christmas Island. Macmillan was unhappy that Kennedy had sanctioned this response to the Soviet testing program without first consulting him.

On 19 May, a gala evening was held at Madison Square Garden to mark Jack's forthcoming forty-fifth birthday. Marilyn Monroe stole the show with her gossamer outfit and breathy rendition of 'Happy Birthday'. Jackie, perhaps fearing that she risked having her nose rubbed into her husband's tawdry affairs, had chosen to attend a horse show in Virginia instead.

Monroe besieged Jack with telephone calls over the following weeks. Bobby's involvement with the star complicated matters still further, and by late June Jack was anxious to sever all relations between her and the Kennedy family.

On Saturday 4 August Monroe telephoned Jack's brother-in-law, Peter Lawford, informing him that she had taken a lot of pills. She died the following day. After a hasty investigation, the police returned a verdict of "probable suicide". Speculation about the exact sequence of events has continued ever since. Bobby is said to have had a stormy encounter with Monroe the day before her death. The other questions surround a possible clean-up operation, in which all material linking Monroe with the Kennedys was removed before the police arrived on the scene, and the speed of the investigation prompted suggestions that the police had been pressured from above.

The summer of 1962 also set in train events which brought the world to the brink of nuclear conflagration. It began in July, when Khrushchev agreed to a request from Castro for military aid. The Soviet leader was sympathetic to Castro's concerns that the US might be planning to invade Cuba. He was also intent on stealing a march on America and getting the upper hand on a president he believed he could dominate. Both Khrushchev and Kennedy knew that the "missile gap", which Jack had warned of during his election campaign, was a complete fiction, it was America who held the military advantage in all departments. Khrushchev knew that placing nuclear warheads on Cuban soil would more than compensate for the overall superiority that the US enjoyed.

Soviet Foreign Minister Andrei Gromyko repeatedly maintained that the weapons build-up was purely a defensive capability. Jack initially gave the Soviet leadership the benefit of the doubt, much to the chagrin of hawkish right-wingers at home. On 15 October a U-2 reconnaissance plane overflew the island and revealed the existence of missile sites with an offensive capability. Jack set up the executive committee of the National Security Council to consider what action the US should take. Over the next two weeks Excomm, whose number included Bobby, Dean Rusk and Robert McNamara, was in session virtually round the clock.

Once the idea of a full-scale invasion of Cuba had been dismissed, two options were on the table: a surgical strike and a blockade. Neither was particularly palatable. The success of a targeted strike could not be guaranteed and would almost certainly lead to an escalation. A blockade would be difficult to enforce and wouldn't address the problem of the forces and the hardware already on the island. It was also dubious in terms of international law.

Jack finally came down in favor of the latter option, neatly sidestepping the legal issue by calling the proposed response a "quarantine line" rather than a blockade.

On 22 October he broadcast to the nation, condemning the Soviet Union's provocative action and making it clear that the US resolve was unshakable. Despite the gravity of the situation, there were a few dissenting voices as the country swung behind its leader. There was also United Nations support, following representations to the Security Council by the American ambassador Adlai Stevenson. Stevenson gave a masterly performance, teasing out denial after denial from the Soviet delegates before dramatically revealing the damning evidence. However, the confrontation was not to be staged in a debating chamber, but on the high seas.

On 24 October two Soviet ships and a submarine approached the quarantine zone. Jack had drawn the line; now he could only wait to see if Khrushchev would cross it. Tensions temporarily eased when the vessels were reported to have turned back. This small victory prompted Rusk's celebrated remark that the enemy had "blinked first".

Jack realized that Khrushchev would not countenance total humiliating defeat. A face-saving compromise was needed. A Soviet withdrawal from Cuba in exchange for a guarantee that the US would not invade the island seemed to have done the trick. But in a

Above: Jackie, pictured during her successful solo trip to India and Pakistan in the sprint of 1962.

subsequent communication from Moscow, Khrushchev added a rider that Jupiter missiles had to be removed from Turkish soil. Kennedy took a calculated gamble. He insisted that the first message should form the basis of the settlement to the immediate crisis, but let it be known that the issue of missiles in Turkey would be addressed in due course. Khrushchev accepted, leaving Castro fuming. In April the following year, when the dust had settled, Jupiter missiles were indeed withdrawn from Turkey.

Jack was applauded for his statesmanship and for keeping a cool head in such a crisis. His approval rating went through the roof, reflected in the strong Democrat showing in the mid-term congressional elections. Others said he'd been very lucky. The hand on the tiller had been uncertain at times, and Kennedy had boxed himself in by imposing the quarantine.

On the domestic front, the burning issue was still civil rights. Despite the unrest of the previous year, Jack still showed great reluctance to act. The celebrated "stroke of the pen" was finally delivered in November 1962. The White

House had been deluged with pens in the mail, a reproachful reminder of the famous election pledge. Civil rights leaders felt that Kennedy had been dragged kicking and screaming to deliver the order, rather than rushing to sign of his own volition. Jack, of course, had one eye on Southern congressmen, whom he had no wish to antagonize.

He had not anguished over the civil rights question in his formative years. This was not out of callous disregard for the plight of those less fortunate; the issue simply didn't touch the privileged life of the young Bostonian. After taking office, things should have been different. But the mature Kennedy was also a hard-nosed politician, and he knew that any action on civil rights was bound to invite praise and vitriol in equal measure.

The perceived tepid action at the top contrasted sharply with white-hot emotions on the ground. They boiled over in September 1962, when twenty-nine-year-old James Meredith attempted to enroll at the all-white University of Mississippi. State Governor Ross Barnett intervened, on the side of the segregationists. He was determined to defy all moves, including a Supreme Court order, to allow Meredith entry to the university. He finally yielded, but as federal marshals escorted Meredith onto the campus, a riot broke out and there were two fatalities. Kennedy emerged with little credit. In their venomous chants the white mob made clear their disgust at White House involvement in the Meredith case. Nor did he impress the likes of Martin Luther King, who felt Kennedy had failed to give a strong moral lead on the issue.

At the end of 1962, however, most Americans focused on Kennedy's handling of the Cuban crisis in assessing the president's second year in office. That Christmas also saw the release of more than a thousand prisoners captured during the Bay of Pigs incident. His stock rose even higher as he met the grateful brigade members at the Miami Orange Bowl. The narrow margin of the election victory over Nixon was now a distant memory. Kennedy gave an upbeat assessment of the previous twelve months, focusing on the US's role in preventing the spread of Communism. Politically he now looked untouchable. Privately, he may have been less enamored with the responsibilities of office. When the Cuban crisis hung perilously in the balance, an exhausted Kennedy had remarked: "If they want this job they can have it, it's no great joy to me".

Opposite: Jack and Jackie at a function, November 1962. As their second year in the White House drew to a close, both enjoyed enormous popularity.

Left: Leaving Mass at Hyannis Port.

Glenn orbits the earth

The beginning of Kennedy's second year in office brought a mixed bag of news. On 13 February the President announced that the release of U2 pilot Gary Powers had been negotiated. Powers had been held by the Soviet Union since May 1960, when his plane was shot down over Soviet air space. A week later, John Glenn became the first American astronaut to orbit the earth. There were difficulties ahead, however. The first American serviceman had been killed in Southeast Asia, and before the year was out, civil rights and Cuba would return to haunt the administration.

Jackie's year of escape

***Above**:* Jackie attends a Democratic Party function to mark her husband's first anniversary as President. This was to be a rare sight in 1962. Having enchanted a host of world leaders the previous year, Jackie would build on those achievements in the following twelve months. This time, however, she would do so without her husband in attendance. There were extended vacations as well as political trips, which meant that the couple spent a considerable amount of time apart.

Left: JFK delivers his second State of the Union address. It outlined thirty-four legislative measures, including increased federal spending on education and medical care for the elderly. He would get fewer than half of his proposals through Congress. Committees packed with Republicans and Southern Democrats would be a constant thorn in his side, particularly in areas of liberal reform.

Below: The President and First Lady welcome the composer Igor Stravinsky to the White House. Occasions such as this reaffirmed Kennedy's stated aim to associate the center of government with high culture. The link between artistic and political freedoms became a recurring theme.

Above: 10 March 1962. Before her delicate visit to meet the Indian and Pakistani heads of state, Jackie stops off at the Vatican. Her audience with Pope John XXIII was also partly diplomatic in nature. Jackie pleaded the case of her sister, Lee, who was seeking an annulment of her first marriage, to Michael Canfield. The church did not recognize their divorce, or Lee's subsequent marriage to Stanislaus Radziwill, which took place in a civil ceremony in 1958. Jackie's intercession had the desired effect, the Vatican agreeing to the annulment in November that year.

Kennedy takes on steel industry

Right: March 1962. Jack receives an honorary degree from the University of California, Berkeley. He was embroiled in a major confrontation with the steel industry at the time. The magnates who ran the corporations eventually buckled under government pressure, rescinding inflationary price rises that Kennedy had described as unjustified. Relationships between the White House and the business community were uneasy thereafter, particularly after Kennedy remarked: "My father always told me that all businessmen were sons-of-bitches but I never believed it till now".

Above: Rose Kennedy has a quiet word with her son during the Joseph P. Kennedy Jr Foundation dinner. Rose met her husband's incapacity with fortitude. Eventually, she delegated the role of primary carer to a niece, Ann Gargan. Joe's condition meant that Jackie had lost her main ally in the family. Her relationship with her mother-in-law remained cordial at best.

US to resume nuclear testing

While Jackie was courting Nehru and Ayub, the premiers of India and Pakistan, Jack had much to occupy him at home. Against his wishes, he felt compelled to authorize the resumption of nuclear testing, the Soviet Union having done so the previous year. This was to be a precursor to a potentially cataclysmic confrontation between the superpowers over Cuba. The civil rights issue was also about to boil over again. Black leaders were still waiting for "the stroke of the pen" with which Kennedy had promised to end discrimination. Away from the affairs of state, Jack was as adventurous as ever. His father's stroke had, if anything, made him even more determined to live for the moment. He duly plunged into an affair with an old college friend, Mary Meyer, which reached new heights of intensity and recklessness.

Diplomatic coup for Jackie

Above: Jackie and her sister enjoy a leisurely form of transportation, Indian style. The First Lady had made a great impression on Jawaharlal Nehru during his visit to Washington the previous fall. Jack had found Nehru difficult, and relations between the two were not helped by India's recent invasion of Goa, a Portuguese colony on the country's west coast. That, together with the fact that the next port of call was to Pakistan, made this no easy baptism for Jackie in her first solo performance on the diplomatic stage. She carried it off with aplomb.

Opposite: Jackie and Lee, pictured at the Radziwills' home in London after completing the successful visit to the subcontinent. Lee effectively acted as Jackie's lady-in-waiting during the trip, and although she executed those duties diligently, she was jealous of the star status accorded her older sister. There was a competitiveness between them which mirrored that between the Kennedy siblings.

Right: Jackie leaves Lee's house in Buckingham Place to attend a dinner at Buckingham Palace, the last official function of her three-week trip. The sisters' relationship survived the fact that Lee was said to be another of Jack's conquests.

Hoover applies pressure

The President hails the returning heroine. Jack was full of praise for Jackie's diplomatic triumph in India and Pakistan. He welcomed her home with a lavish reception as an acknowledgment of her achievements. He was also extremely indulgent when Jackie asked him to make speedy arrangements for the importation of Sardar, a magnificent horse presented to her by Pakistan's Prime Minister Ayub Khan. Even as he was displaying such open affection, Jack was maneuvering behind the scenes to protect himself from J. Edgar Hoover's attentions. On 22 March, a week before Jackie's return, the FBI chief informed the President that he was aware of the affair between him and Judith Campbell, and that Campbell was also the mistress of Mafia boss Sam Giancana. This was not the only piece of salacious information Hoover had on Kennedy, which was undoubtedly the reason Jack kept him on when he took office. He had no wish to make an enemy of Hoover, and quickly severed all ties with Campbell.

"Happy Birthday Mr President"

Above: Jack and Bobby flank New York Mayor Robert Wagner as he announces an initiative to deal with juvenile delinquency. Jack described the problem as "a matter which requires action by us all". Two weeks earlier, unruly New York teenagers had been the furthest thing from Jack's mind. On 19 May he attended a Democratic Party function at Madison Square Garden, which was both a fund-raiser and an advanced celebration of his 45th birthday. It was at this event that Marilyn Monroe, attired in a gossamer, skintight gown, appeared on stage to sing 'Happy Birthday'. The performance was so sultry and provocative that journalist Dorothy Kilgallen likened it to "making love to the president in direct view of 40 million Americans".

Jack had first met Monroe in November 1961. Given his weakness for beautiful women and Hollywood glamor, the affair was hardly surprising. Monroe invested more in the relationship than Jack did, even entertaining hopes that he might leave Jackie and marry her. Jackie was spared her overtly sexual Madison Square Garden performance, choosing instead to attend a Virginia horse show with Caroline.

Opposite: Jack pitches the first ball of the 1962 baseball season, following a presidential tradition dating back to the time of William Taft.

Ransom agreed for Bay of Pigs hostages

Above: Enjoying a family break at Palm Springs, Easter 1962. Jack was engaged in behind-the-scenes negotiations to secure the release of those captured during the Bay of Pigs invasion. At first he was determined not to yield to Castro's huge ransom demands. That would have been at odds with the high standards of integrity he had said would characterize his administration. Ultimately, however, the pragmatist in him won through. He finally agreed to pay $56 million in cash and goods to secure the release of more than a thousand prisoners.

Opposite: Jackie shows off John Jr to the Empress of Iran during a state visit, April 1962. Kennedy and Khrushchev had held up Iran as an example in a heated exchange on the cause of revolution during their Vienna summit. Khrushchev argued that it was United States' backing of reactionary governments that was responsible for most regime changes. Jack's riposte was that autocratic leaders such as the Shah would have to change or be forced aside if they failed to improve the lot of their people. The Soviet leader had the better of the debate, though Jack's words were prescient as far as Iran was concerned.

"Special Relationship" under strain

Opposite: 28 April 1962. The Kennedys return to Washington to prepare for the visit of Harold Macmillan. Lady Dorothy did not accompany Britain's premier, so Jackie did not have the usual commitments for a visiting head of state. Relations between Kennedy and Macmillan remained good, although they disagreed over nuclear testing. Macmillan urged Kennedy to show restraint in the hope of securing a test ban agreement with the Soviet Union. Jack authorized the resumption of testing without consulting Macmillan, incurring the latter's anger. Even so, many of Kennedy's senior advisers were concerned that he was being unduly influenced by his British counterpart.

Above: Jack was fond of gadgets, particularly telecommunications technology. In the Oval Office he had an 18-button telephone installed, through which he conducted a lot of presidential business. He is pictured sending a signal from Palm Beach via satellite to officially open the 1962 World's Fair in Seattle.

Concerns over Soviet arms in Cuba

4 May 1962. Jack, surrounded by some of the top brass during a military display at Eglin Air Base, Florida. American forces would soon be on a war footing. The early months of 1962 had seen a steady stream of Soviet military personnel and weaponry flow into Cuba. Jack and his advisers kept the situation under review, and were prepared to tolerate the build-up, provided it was only a defensive capability. The First Lady continued to spend much of her time away from her husband. In early May she paid a surprise visit to her father-in-law, who was attempting his first steps since suffering a stroke six months earlier.

Political power and high culture

Left: The worsening situation in Laos was the theme of this news conference, held on 9 May 1962. Kennedy announced that Communist forces were continuing to make inroads into the country, a clear breach of the cease-fire agreement. Two months later, in July 1962, both the United States and Soviet Union endorsed the Geneva Accords, which established a neutralist government under Prince Souvanna Phouma. Under its terms, all external factions were to withdraw. In fact, the war merely became a covert operation. Hanoi continued its support of the Communist Pathet Lao, while the US initiated a counterinsurgency program. With Kennedy's approval, the CIA recruited thousands of Laotian tribesmen who acted as guerrilla warriors.

Above: In formal attire for one of the many gala dinners that the President and First Lady held at the White House. Jackie was the driving force behind such occasions, and the guest list included Tennessee Williams, Arthur Miller, Pablo Casals, Leonard Bernstein and Mark Rothko. Jack's cultural interests were somewhat more low-brow, and he occasionally had to be prompted as to which field the visitors excelled in. On one such occasion, a dinner given in honor of a host of Nobel Prize winners, Jack remarked: "I think that this is the most extraordinary collection of human knowledge that has ever been gathered together at the White House - with the possible exception of when Thomas Jefferson dined alone".

The Oval Office as playground

Right: The Oval Office was not off-limits to the Kennedy children. Jack encouraged them to come and play in the 35ft by 28ft room that was the seat of power. Here, in May 1962, he delights in seeing John Jr take some of his first faltering steps. Jack is sitting on the desk Jackie rescued from an unused room when they took up residence at the White House. Made from the timbers of HMS *Resolute*, it was presented to President Rutherford Hayes by Queen Victoria in 1878. The naval theme was continued with several artifacts, including the coconut shell on which Jack wrote his famous SOS message during the survival ordeal of 1943.

Left: Jack and Jackie show a united front as they receive delegates to a Democratic Women's conference at the White House. It was shortly after Marilyn Monroe's show-stopping performance, and the actress was now bombarding the White House with calls day and night. Jackie herself is said to have received one of these impassioned messages. As was her custom, the First Lady met the inevitable gossip and speculation with serene dignity.

Below: The President and First Lady greet the American Ballet Company before they give a performance at the Executive Mansion. Jackie was at her husband's side at a number of engagements in the week following Monroe's Madison Square Garden performance. At one banquet she wore a gown not dissimilar to the one in which Monroe had caused such a sensation. Jackie had recently hosted a dinner in which playwright Arthur Miller was one of the honored guests. Miller, one of the victims of the McCarthy witch hunts, had just remarried after divorcing Monroe.

Jackie's restoration triumph

Right: Jackie shows off the newly restored Treaty Room. One of the most historic in the White House, it first served as the Cabinet room during Lincoln's presidency. At the end of Jackie's grand restoration of the White House, she hosted a television program in which she described the improvements and acquisitions. Ever mindful of the public relations angle, Jack was apprehensive about the venture, but Jackie carried it off impressively.

Above: Setting off on a three-day goodwill visit to Mexico, 29 June 1962. It had been almost a month since the last official White House function of the season. For that final engagement, Jack had brazenly invited Mary Meyer, a situation reminiscent of the way Joe invited Gloria Swanson to accompany him and his wife on an overseas trip more than 30 years earlier. Meyer's presence at a White House dinner, coming on top of the Monroe affair, made Jackie seek the sanctuary of Glen Ora. She spent most of the following month at the country retreat, returning to Washington shortly before the official visit to Mexico.

Opposite: The Kennedys receive a rapturous welcome in Mexico City. The trip was a triumph. Jackie won everybody over with her beauty and elegance, not to mention an address delivered in perfect Spanish. It was a charm offensive which also gave out a clear political signal to Cuba - and the Soviet Union - that Mexico was firmly in the pro-Western, democratic family.

Drugs at the White House

Above: Rose Kennedy assumes the role of consort for an official visit by Ecuador's head of state, Julio Arosemena. Press reports made much of the First Lady's absence. Jackie, asserting her independence, felt she had performed for enough statesmen over the last year and chose to remain at Hyannis Port. With a major crisis looming, Jack was experimenting with various drugs. In addition to Novocaine and cortisone, he was introduced to amphetamines by Max Jacobson, the guru to the rich and famous known as Dr Feel Good.

Opposite: After a nine-month-long White House social season peppered with cultural events, watching a baseball game comes as something of a relief. The summer months brought increasing concerns over the build-up of Soviet forces in Cuba, although Jack remained unconvinced that this constituted a threat. He focused a lot of attention on the mid-term congressional election campaign, frustrated that so many legislative measures were being blocked. After months of supporting the President in her official capacity - and helping boost his popularity - Jackie sought sanctuary away from the limelight. In August she took Caroline to Ravello, Italy, where the Radziwills had rented a villa. Mary Meyer was a regular visitor to the White House in her absence.

First Lady's vacation irks President - and voters

Left: Ravello offered no escape from the world's press, who were out in force to get a shot of the First Lady. Pictures of her in a bathing costume raised eyebrows at home as some Americans felt it was undignified for a woman in her position. The coverage got even worse for Jackie when she was reported to be spending a lot of time in the company of Gianni Agnelli, one of the jet-setters who was in the vacation party. Jack was more annoyed with the political fall-out than the suggestion of any impropriety. He cabled Jackie the terse instruction: "Less Agnelli, more Caroline".

Opposite: Jack at work in the Oval Office, late August 1962. He was irked by Jackie's decision to extend her vacation in Italy. Many American voters were too, particularly women's groups who felt she was abdicating her responsibilities by cavorting in foreign climes when her place was at home supporting the President. Jack responded by insisting that Jackie and Caroline return home before the end of the month. She took him at his word, arriving at Newport on 31 August.

Below: Jackie pictured with Lee Radziwill during their vacation in Italy. The culture, company and recreational activities were a world away from those of the Kennedy compound at Hyannis Port.

LBJ's loathing for deputy's role

Jack visits Cape Canaveral, where he meets the first American to orbit the earth, Colonel John Glenn. Kennedy had awarded Glenn the Distinguished Service Medal for the historic flight on *Friendship* 7 in February 1962. Hovering in the background is vice-president Lyndon Johnson. Johnson hated the role, in which he felt emasculated. Having relinquished the power base he enjoyed as Senate leader, he had little executive authority in the Kennedy administration. Diplomatic visits overseas would be the highlights of his tenure in the No 2 job.

"The new frontier of science and space"

Above: 12 September 1962. In a speech at Rice University, Texas, Jack reaffirms his vision for the United States to lead the world in space technology, and the objective of reaching the moon before the end of the decade. Houston would be at the center of this technological revolution: "What was once the farthest outpost on the old frontier of the West will be the farthest outpost on the new frontier of science and space".

Opposite: Newport, Rhode Island, 14 September 1962. Jackie, at a dinner to mark the finals of the America's Cup. She and the children spent most of the month at Hammersmith Farm. On 12 September Jack flew from Washington to join her as they celebrated their 9th wedding anniversary. On top of the negative press reports concerning Jackie's vacation, rumors began to circulate that in 1947 Jack had been briefly married to a woman named Durie Malcolm.

Left: Jackie, accompanied by John D. Rockefeller III at the opening of the Philharmonic Hall at the Lincoln Center.

The President and First Lady are keen observers as the United States yacht *Weatherley* takes on *Gretel*, Australia's vessel, in the first of the races for the 1962 America's Cup. Yachting was a passion for Jack, and this was the first America's Cup competition during his presidency. With the Cuba crisis deepening by the day, his vacation included regular briefings from Washington. He managed to see America retain the trophy before the confrontation with the Soviet Union demanded his round-the-clock attention.

Riots as black student enrolls in Mississippi

30 September 1962. The President delivers a broadcast to try to defuse the volatile situation surrounding James Meredith's enrollment at the University of Mississippi. Meredith, a 29-year-old black ex-serviceman, had been inspired by Kennedy's inaugural address and applied to enter his home state's university. When he was rejected, he took his case to court, eventually winning on appeal. Mississippi's governor, Ross Barnett, expressed his intention to defy the ruling. An internecine domestic conflict was the last thing Jack wanted at such a time, but he gave the order for federal troops to be deployed. He broadcast to the nation as Meredith was being escorted onto the campus. Two speeches were prepared, depending on whether the enrollment had been carried out peacefully or not. Even as he began reading the speech suggesting the situation in Oxford was calm, violence erupted. There were many casualties and two fatalities. Kennedy was applauded for what was seen as his determination to uphold one individual's rights. Black leaders were less impressed, feeling that Kennedy was still dragging his heels on civil rights legislation.

Jack and Bobby discuss the consequences of the recent violence in Mississippi. The Attorney General had made a series of telephone calls to Governor Barnett. At one point a deal was struck to allow Meredith to register. When Barnett changed his mind, Bobby threatened to go public on the governor's duplicity. Knowing that such revelations would damage him irreparably in the state, Barnett reluctantly capitulated. This was a classic example of Bobby's steely resolve and readiness to "play hardball".

Missile sites threaten United States

Above: The President entertains a delegation of Soviet officials, including Foreign Minister Andrei Gromyko (second right). The two superpowers were still posturing when this meeting took place, on 18 October. Three days earlier, a U2 reconnaissance plane had revealed missile sites which had an offensive capability, giving the lie to the Soviet line that the weapons were there purely for defensive reasons. Jack had the photographic evidence in his drawer during the two-hour meeting.

Left: The burden of office is clearly depicted as JFK agonizes over the United States' response to the missile sites on Cuba. On 20 October he informed the American people of the gravity of the situation, and said that if the Soviet Union did not begin dismantling the sites within 48 hours, a quarantine line would be placed around Cuba. This was effectively a blockade, but that term was not used as it was a potential breach of international law.

Cuban Missile Crisis

Opposite: The US government faces an agonizing wait until the deadline, 10 a.m. on 24 October. In his broadcast Kennedy had called on Khrushchev "to halt and eliminate this clandestine, reckless and provocative threat to world peace". Concerned that the Soviet leader would choose war, Jack had asked Jackie to place herself and the children in the nuclear bunker. She refused.

Above: West German Chancellor Konrad Adenauer delivers a speech, with JFK and Secretary of State Dean Rusk looking on. As the Cuban situation hung in the balance, the United States sent emissaries to several European countries to garner support. Adenauer, along with France's President de Gaulle, strongly backed America's position.

Left: The popularity of the President and First Lady soars in the wake of the Cuban missile crisis. The Soviet Union shied away from crossing the line that had been drawn, which was seen as a personal triumph for Jack. Jackie had given her husband total support in the darkest moments. Now, the cracks in the relationship were revealed once again. Jack invited Mary Meyer to a celebratory dinner at the White House and they also clashed over a new house on Rattlesnake Mountain, Atoka, Virginia. For Jackie it was a dream property. Jack hated it.

Riding high in the polls

Opposite: 19 November 1962. While Jackie enjoys a day's riding with the children, Jack follows up his political coup over Cuba by delivering the long awaited "stroke of the pen". This outlawed discrimination in federally assisted housing, a tentative first step on the civil rights agenda. Late 1962 also saw progress on the issue of weapons inspections, which had been a stumbling block between the United States and the Soviet Union as far as a nuclear test ban treaty was concerned. The year ended with a fanfare at Miami's Orange Bowl, where Jack and Jackie were feted in front of the 1113 Cuban exiles whose release the President had negotiated. All these achievements played well with the electorate, and the Democrats were rewarded at the ballot box in the mid-term congressional elections.

Above: The Kennedys spent Christmas 1962 at Palm Beach, where they received the news that Joe's condition had worsened. He developed pneumonia, and on 24 December an emergency tracheotomy was performed to relieve his breathing. Jackie is pictured leaving the hospital after visiting her father-in-law. Meanwhile, Jack was as cavalier as ever. Two weeks earlier he had spent the weekend at the Bing Crosby estate at Palm Springs, where Peter Lawford, as usual, provided plenty of female company.

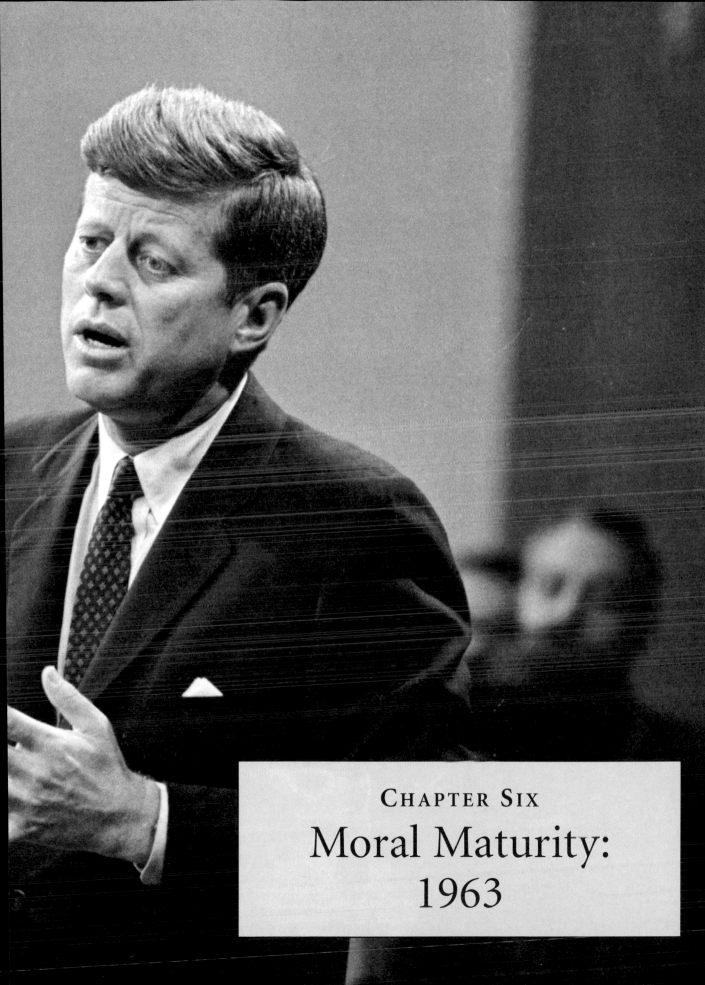

CHAPTER SIX
Moral Maturity: 1963

The beginning of 1963 was very different for the President and the First Lady. Jack was riding high in the opinion polls and was enjoying better health than he had for some time. He was also still conducting his affair with Mary Meyer. Jackie, by contrast, was at a low ebb. She discovered she was pregnant again, the joy tempered by concern over a possible miscarriage or complications. Even before the pregnancy was confirmed, she had decided to rein back her public duties. The rally at the Miami Orange Bowl at the end of 1962 would be the last event on such a scale that she would attend with her husband until the fateful trip to Dallas 11 months later. The refurbishment of the White House was largely complete, and there would be a void to fill. But in the past two years she felt she had discharged her PR duties as the President's consort. To the outside world he was now looking every inch the mature statesman. With her husband's image firmly established, Jackie saw it as no great hardship to leave the stage to him. She had no great fondness for the role of First Lady, and even the the very term raised her hackles.

Her mood would not have been helped by the fact that Jack's affair with Meyer had been made public in a drunken outburst by a newspaperman at a press convention. Although it was kept out of print, the affair was now in the public domain. Jackie was well versed in remaining aloof from casual liaisons based purely on sex. This was something more, and thus more hurtful. Things came to a head in March. Jack decided to end his relationship with Meyer, although he would be drawn back to her within a matter of weeks.

If domestic calm had been restored, temporarily at least, Jack's administration was about to be rocked by the worst civil unrest ever seen on America's streets. He was engaged in a battle of wills with Congress over his budget plans to stimulate the economy with a $13.5 billion tax cut. The US was already running a sizeable deficit, and his proposals had not met with universal approval. Fiscal policy soon became a secondary issue as blacks throughout the country took their frustration onto the streets. Even the usually moderate tones of Martin Luther King became markedly more incensed at the lack of government action.

Alabama was the flash point. Under the governorship of arch-segregationist George Wallace, it was the only state which refused to countenance integration at its state university in Tuscaloosa. On 11 June, Wallace reluctantly stood aside to allow black students Vivian Malone and James Hood to enter the building, but made it clear that this was the loss of a battle, not the war.

That same evening, Jack made a ground-breaking speech. He announced that far-reaching civil rights legislation would be put before Congress within a matter of days. This was a lot more than just a policy statement, though. For the first time, he embraced the moral dimension of the issue, as King and others had long urged him to do. He invoked the Constitution itself, in which the equality of all individuals was a core tenet. The content of the speech and the passion with which it was delivered was thought to be too dangerous a cocktail by some of his advisers. Kennedy ignored them, but he knew that presenting a civil rights bill to Congress and seeing it enacted were two very different things. The riots continued, with demonstrators unwilling to show the restraint Kennedy had called for. Medgar Evers, a member of the National Association for the Advancement of

Colored People, was murdered in Jackson, Mississippi. A week later, on the day of Evers' funeral, Kennedy's bill was presented before Congress. In his supporting speech he spoke of the graveyards of the battlefields being color-blind. It was reminiscent of how he had defused the Catholic issue on the campaign trail by noting that nobody had asked him or his brother about their religious beliefs when they fought for their country.

On 28 August, more than 200,000 gathered at the Lincoln Memorial to hear an address by Dr King. He, too, referred to the Constitution, citing the famous words "We hold these truths to be self-evident, that all men are created equal". But his refrain, and his "dream", was that the fine words would be reflected in everyday society.

Despite the outstanding oratory of both men, the civil rights bill still hung in the balance in November 1963. It would eventually be passed in July the following year. It was left to Lyndon Johnson to preside over wide-ranging measures to end discrimination on grounds of race, color, sex and religion. Naturally, Kennedy would receive much posthumous credit for this landmark piece of legislation. However, some maintain that its successful passage was predicated on the wave of emotion which followed his assassination.

On 10 June, the day before Kennedy spoke to the nation of the moral imperative of the civil rights issue, he made another keynote address. The venue was American University, Washington, the theme was the "peace race". During the Cuban crisis the previous fall, Jack had been made fully aware of the hidden danger of radioactive fallout. This made him redouble his efforts to secure a test ban treaty with Khrushchev, ignoring advisers who thought it would accomplish little, other than deliver a potentially fatal blow to his hopes of re-election. Harold Macmillan had urged Jack to put morality before personal popularity or political gain, and in the memorable American University speech he did just that. Two months later, the two most powerful men on the planet agreed to establish a hot-line connection between them. The Cuban crisis had revealed an inadequate and potentially dangerous system of communication between the two superpowers. Jack wanted to ensure that future security could not be jeopardized by poor communications.

The test ban treaty was finally signed on 7 October, 1963. Although it excluded underground testing, it was nevertheless an important first step in halting the arms race, and stands as one of Kennedy's greatest achievements.

Relations between the superpowers were now less frosty, but only because of a shared understanding that the policy of Mutual Assured Destruction presented a cataclysmic threat to the present generation, and cast a long shadow over those to come. In terms of ideology, there was accommodation, not reconciliation. Jack made that perfectly clear when he visited West Berlin during a 10-day tour of Europe at the end of June. He was visibly moved by seeing the Berlin Wall for the first time. It was a symbol of repression and subjugation, and he made freedom his theme: "All free men, wherever they may live, are citizens of Berlin, and therefore, as a free man, I take pride in the words 'Ich bin ein Berliner'".

On 7 August, Jackie was rushed to hospital, where she underwent an emergency Cesarean. Patrick Bouvier Kennedy was born five weeks premature. He suffered from the same respiratory problem that had afflicted John and died two days later. Jack had arrived at the hospital too late for the birth, but it was he who held the baby's hand as he lost the fight for life. Jack had shielded Jackie from the gravity of the situation. He now faced her as a distraught father. In keeping with the new-found moral perspective which now underpinned his political life, his reaction to the loss of a third child took on a new dimension. The contrast with the events of 1956 was stark. Jack's outpouring seems to have been a mixture of grief and guilt. The tragedy undoubtedly brought them closer than they had been for a long time.

In the fall of 1963, concern over events in Southeast Asia rose to the top of the political agenda. Jack had continued Eisenhower's policy of supporting South Vietnam's anti-Communist government, headed by Ngo Dinh Diem. Until now he had focused much of his attention on Cuba, Berlin and Moscow. The persecution of Buddhists by the corrupt Catholic government changed all that, and presented Kennedy with a dilemma. He was worried about the inroads the Viet Cong were making, and the possibility of the country falling to Communism. But he could not sanction the brutality of the Diem regime. Shocking pictures of Buddhist monks who chose self-immolation over repression flashed round the world. Kennedy was receiving mixed messages from his advisers. Some recommended a full-scale military solution, while Jack inclined to those who had grave reservations about expanding the US's involvement.

Above: Jack preferred sport to high culture. Golf became a passion, although he was invariably hampered by his back problem.

The South Vietnamese authorities were exhorted to clean up their act and to halt the oppression. When this fell on deaf ears, regime change emerged as an increasingly desirable outcome. Jack, still grieving over the death of his son and concerned over Jackie's well-being, was informed that a military coup in South Vietnam was a real possibility. The rebel general wanted US approval before acting, and Jack gave the green light, provided his top aides had no objection. Some of those advisers, including Secretary of State Dean Rusk, did indeed have objections, but deferred to what they believed was the President's view. Only after the plan was sanctioned did the

misunderstanding come to light. Kennedy desperately tried to withdraw his approval, but the momentum was now unstoppable. The coup finally took place on 1 November. Jack was worried that the insurrection might be laid at the US's door, putting the improved relations with the Soviet Union at risk. Publicly, it was important to distance America from events in South Vietnam.

Jack at least wanted Diem and his supporters to be treated with dignity, but matters were now out of his hands. He was appalled when he learned that Diem and his brother, Ngo Dinh Nhu, had been murdered. The immediate impact on the President was a powerful sense

of personal responsibility. Since his father had become incapacitated, Jack had been much influenced by Macmillan, particularly when the exigencies of office brought morality and expediency into conflict. It is doubtful whether Joe Sr would have anguished about Diem's fate.

In the fall of 1963 Jack's conduct as both President and husband could still be called into question. Indecisiveness and lack of judgment over Vietnam mirrored events surrounding the Bay of Pigs debacle. And despite his tender concerns over Jackie, he still couldn't give up Mary Meyer. But at least he could now recognize a

grievous wrong, both in his public and private life, and had the capacity to feel remorse and guilt.

How Kennedy would have dealt with the long-term ramifications of the coup in Vietnam remains a matter of conjecture. Some suggest he was intent on scaling back US military involvement in the country, others that he passionately believed in maintaining a strong presence in the area, and that his commitment to winning the war was unshakable. One thing is clear. Following the events of 22 November, the new President and his advisory team didn't appear to make any radical policy changes regarding US involvement in Southeast

Asia. Under Johnson, there was a huge escalation of American forces in this theater. It thus seems reasonable to suggest that JFK may have presided over a similar military build-up had he lived.

Jack's thoughts turned to the forthcoming election. Formulating policy on Southeast Asia or in any other area was academic if a second term could not be secured. Put another way, the pragmatist in him came to the fore. The domestic economy was in good shape. In his handling of the Cold War and civil rights he had managed to enhance his credentials with the Left without alienating the Right. Vietnam was another potential banana skin, but he calculated that this issue could be held in abeyance without causing him significant electoral damage. Overall,

conditions were favorable for another successful campaign, with Barry Goldwater his likely opponent.

A two-day visit to Texas was planned, one of the first ports of call in the long re-election campaign. A row had broken out between two leading Democrats, Governor John Connally and Senator Ralph Yarborough. Jack saw the visit as an opportunity to heal the rift between the two men, and to kickstart the 1964 campaign.

It had been a long time since Jackie had accompanied her husband on a domestic political trip. Seeing how badly affected Jack had been by Diem's assassination, she decided to join him on the visit to Texas. It would be her first visit to the Lone Star state. It would be her husband's last.

Left: At the Berlin Wall, 26 June 1963. Jack made his famous "Ich bin ein Berliner" speech in Rudolf Wilde Platz the same day.

Below: Jack stands shoulder to shoulder with West Berlin's mayor, Willy Brandt, and Germany's Chancellor Konrad Adenauer. His unequivocal commitment to guarantee the divided city's freedom was greeted with rapturous enthusiasm by its people.

A new dimension

Opposite above: The President ushers in the new year with a reception for labor and civil rights leaders, including Martin Luther King. Jack was riding high in the opinion polls at the end of his second year in office. Until now his instincts had been to consolidate support and avoid risk. This year would be different. 1963 would see policy initiatives informed by a new moral dimension, even though he knew such actions jeopardized his chances of re-election.

Opposite below: 14 January 1963. Jackie watches her husband deliver his third State of the Union address, along with her mother, Janet Auchinloss, and sister Princess Lee Radziwill. For Jackie the year began on a joyous note as she discovered she was pregnant again. Having lost two babies, the happiness was tempered with trepidation. She was especially concerned in the early weeks of pregnancy, and the announcement was not made official until mid-April.

Above: Jack in ebullient mood as he outlines his views on how long politicians should be allowed to serve in office. He was already giving thought to what he would do after his days in the White House were over. One idea was for the creation of the John F. Kennedy Presidential Library at Harvard, and he was already having discussions with his alma mater about this prestigious project.

The price of glamor

Opposite: At a state dinner for the visit of Venezuela's president Romulo Betancourt, Jackie's hairstyle receives as much attention as any political utterances. As usual, women throughout the country quickly copied any new look that Jackie adopted. The appearance came at a price, however. Designer outfits contributed to the $226,000 bill she ran up in her first two years as First Lady. Jack was not best pleased and insisted that her spending was reined in, even though he was estimated to be worth $10 million at the time.

Above: Jackie enjoys a night out at the theater with her sister and brother-in-law. The First Lady decided to drastically curtail her public engagements in 1963. After two years of notable achievement in discharging her duties, Jackie was keen to leave the stage to her husband. Pregnancy offered her the ideal excuse to make family considerations her main priority.

Left: Jack confers with Ted Sorensen, the man behind many of the memorable words Jack had spoken during the previous decade. Sorensen would soon be called upon to draft major speeches on civil rights and nuclear arms reduction, which would have the same kind of impact as the Inaugural Address of 1961.

Letter to Khruschev

Opposite: 24 April 1963. Jack announces a breakthrough in the stalled negotiations with the Soviet Union over nuclear testing. Harold Macmillan had written to Kennedy a month earlier, urging him to do all he could to break the deadlock. The pressures on Jack were huge, both from the hawkish tendency within his own party as well as the Republican opposition. Even if a treaty could be agreed, there was no guarantee that Congress would ratify it. Jack put these considerations aside, and both he and Macmillan were co-signatories to a letter sent to Khruschev, indicating their willingness to resume talks.

Above: The President and First Lady enjoy a motorcade journey through Washington to mark the state visit of the King of Morocco. Jackie needed all her skills as a public performer for the visit, as she was in turmoil at the time. Jack's affair with Mary Meyer had been revealed in a drunken outburst by journalist Phil Graham at a press convention in Phoenix. This liaison caused Jackie increasing pain, as it went beyond the casual encounters which she had always tolerated.

The President exudes confidence as he fields journalists' questions at a news conference, April 1963. Jack had been studying a report documenting a century of struggle for America's black population. It was a shameful history of egregious acts of discrimination, much of it institutional. When many prominent black figures were invited to a White House reception, Jack showed he was still apprehensive about the issue. Sammy Davis Jr, entertainer and member of the famous a "Rat Pack", attended with his Swedish wife, May Britt. Interracial marriages were still regarded by many as taboo, and Jack took care to ensure that the couple didn't pose together for the photographers.

Racial violence in Alabama

Opposite below: 12 May 1963. The President calls for calm as the tinderbox of Alabama threatens to ignite in a race war. Civil rights campaigners had been holding demonstrations in the state for the past month, protesting over blatant discriminatory policies that were endorsed by its arch-segregationist governor, George Wallace. Kennedy made it clear that if order was not restored, federal troops would be deployed.

Above: Jackie was keen to make an impact when she played hostess to the Grand Duke and Duchess of Luxembourg at the end of April. It was to be the last such White House reception she would preside over as First Lady before the birth of her baby. She invited the actor Basil Rathbone to put on a special performance, requesting him to recite the St Crispin's Day speech from *Henry the Fifth*, a favorite of Jack's.

Opposite above: Bobby Kennedy and J. Edgar Hoover deep in consultation, with a major scandal brewing. Both men became aware that one of the President's casual partners, Ellen Rometsch, was also involved with a Soviet attaché. It was potentially as damaging as the Profumo affair which was currently rocking the British government to its foundations. Jack quickly dropped Rometsch and she was subsequently deported. As late as fall 1963 RFK and Hoover were putting pressure on senators who were demanding an investigation into the affair. Had it not been for the events of 22 November, the Rometsch scandal may have dealt a serious blow to the Kennedy administration.

Jack and Jackie shared a passion for history, particularly the American Civil War. In the spring of 1963 they visited a number of historic sites, including Gettysburg, Pennsylvania, where they engaged in typical good-humored banter as to whose knowledge of the period was greater. For some three months Jackie was buoyed by the thought that her husband had ended his relationship with Mary Meyer. She also had the fillip of moving the family out of the "Kennedy compound" at Hyannis Port, which she had never liked. Their new home on Cape Cod was Brambletyde, Squaw Island, some half a mile away from the compound. Jack liked the property, chiefly because of its proximity to the ocean. He was less taken with Jackie's other pet project, their new house in Virginia. He was also angry that having spent a lot of money redecorating Glen Ora, they had to pay a huge sum to restore it to its original condition when the lease was up.

President invokes Constitution on civil rights issue

Left: 18 May 1963. Jack meets Peace Corps workers bound for Indonesia. The Peace Corps remained one of the administration's success stories, and Kennedy's interest in international affairs was undiminished. However, the wave of violence in Alabama occupied his thoughts, and later the same day he gave an impassioned speech on civil rights at Vanderbilt University, Tennessee. The rioting continued, and there were shocking pictures of the police turning their dogs loose on the protestors, a move sanctioned by Police Chief "Bull" Connors. Kennedy responded by invoking the Constitution itself, which held equality as a core tenet. A civil rights bill was drafted and put before Congress the following month.

Opposite: Jackie's renovation of the White House included a lot of work on the grounds, especially the Rose Garden. As a surprise gift for their forthcoming tenth anniversary, Jackie began work on a scrapbook of the restoration work.

Above: Jackie introduces John Jr to astronaut Gordon Cooper, who had just been presented with the Distinguished Service Medal at a White House ceremony. John Jr was fascinated by flight. When Jack's helicopter landed, father and son would often spend time playing at the controls together. Kite flying was another favorite pastime, and Jack kept toy planes in the Oval Office for when his son came to play. Jackie was the inspiration behind Caroline's main passion, horseriding.

The White House school

Above: Jackie and Caroline at the White House kindergarten, late spring 1963. Jackie was heavily involved in the setting up of the school, keen to give her children as normal an upbringing as possible. It eventually had ten pupils and was staffed by regular teachers. The public loved domestic images of the First Family, and there was huge media interest in Jackie's pregnancy. The fall would see a dramatic turnaround, with Jackie subjected to some vitriolic abuse from both the press and the public.

Opposite: Jackie and John Jr with other Kennedy family members at the White House, 24 May 1963. Five days later, in celebration of Jack's 46th birthday, Jackie organized a trip down the Potomac on the yacht *Sequoia*. Mary Meyer joined the party, something Jackie accepted with equanimity as Meyer was now the mistress of one of Jack's aides. She would be devastated shortly afterwards when it became clear that Jack had resumed his affair with her.

Below: The arrival of the presidential helicopter, Marine One, holds up a baseball game between some of the White House aides and members of the Senate Foreign Relations staff. The White House team included press secretary Pierre Salinger (left) and Ted Sorensen (right). Salinger fronted the daily press briefings and was an important conduit for making the business of government more accessible than it had been in previous administrations.

Left: 30 May 1963. Rose Kennedy, pictured at a street bearing her eldest son's name, part of a Memorial Day service at Fort Banks, Winthrop, Massachusetts.

Khruschev agrees to test ban talks

Above: The President tracks a missile launched at the White Sands missile range. Shortly afterwards, Khrushchev gave a positive reply to the letter he and Macmillan had sent, and it was agreed that high-level talks between the superpowers would take place in July. The news came through during a five-day domestic trip which included a visit to Texas. There he met Governor John Connally and Senator Ralph Yarborough, the protagonists in some bitter in-fighting between rival Democratic factions. The differences between the two were unresolved, and Jack agreed to return to the Lone Star state before the end of the year.

"Ich bin ein Berliner"

Opposite below: 26 June 1963. Jack addresses a huge West Berlin crowd at Rudolf Wilde Platz. His speech contrasted democracy and freedom with the repression of Communist regimes: "Freedom has many difficulties and democracy is not perfect, but we have never had to put a wall up to keep our people in, to prevent them from leaving us". He pointed out that freedom was absolute, not relative, and the subjugation of one man was a denial of freedom to all: "All free men, wherever they may live, are citizens of Berlin, and therefore, as a free man, I take pride in the words Ich bin ein Berliner".

Opposite above: Against the backdrop of the Brandenburg Gate, the Presidential party, including Robert and Ethel Kennedy and West Berlin's mayor, Willy Brandt, gets a first-hand view of the Berlin Wall, constructed two years earlier. The East Berlin authorities draped the arches of the famous portal in red cloth to prevent the dignitaries from looking into their territory.

Above: The President fields questions at a press conference in Bonn, 25 June 1963. He reaffirms his unwavering support for West Berlin. The sight of the Wall had affected him deeply, bringing his "cold warrior" instincts to the fore.

Ireland welcomes a son

Opposite: After the highly charged political visit to Germany, the next leg of Kennedy's European tour had more personal resonance. There were chaotic scenes in Cork, Ireland, where the people turned out in droves to catch a glimpse of a world leader whose roots lay in their homeland.

Left: Mary Ryan, a distant relative of Jack's, steps up to plant a kiss on the presidential cheek. At one point, when the crush threatened to become overwhelming, security men stepped forward to intervene. Jack waved them away with the words "It's all right, these are my people".

Below: Jack and his sister, Eunice Shriver, visit the ancestral home of the Kennedy clan in Dunganstown, County Wexford. It was from here that Jack's great-grandfather Patrick Kennedy had emigrated to the United States in 1848. Jackie tried to incorporate the Kennedy roots into their new home in Virginia, renaming it "Wexford".

Jack was a keen if not very accomplished golfer. Back pain often restricted his ability to play, but in July 1963 he was feeling better than he had for some time. He spent much of the month at Brambletyde, where Jackie was filling her time reading and painting while awaiting the birth of their child. The brazen way in which Jack had renewed his affair with Mary Meyer hit Jackie hard. It appeared as deliberate and callous as the way in which Joe Kennedy flaunted his mistresses before Rose. He was also a concerned expectant father, however, and Jackie became even more anxious that her pregnancy should proceed normally.

Previous page: 19 July 1963. A family gathering at Hyannis Port to mark the christening of the newest family member. Patricia Lawford holds Christopher George Kennedy, Bobby and Ethel's eighth child, who had been christened by Cardinal Richard Cushing at St Francis Xavier Church. Jack was looking forward to repeating the ceremony after the birth of his third child. In the meantime, he was preoccupied by the nuclear test ban talks, which had begun in Moscow four days earlier. Underground testing looked like being the sticking point, and Jack instructed his envoy, Averell Harriman, to secure a deal just on atmospheric testing if a total ban wasn't possible. Macmillan had urged this course of action as a very worthy second prize. Agreement was finally reached at the end of the month.

Opposite above: Jackie, seven months pregnant, takes the strain out of accompanying her husband around the golf course at Newport, Rhode Island. She had already begun organizing the baby's room and making arrangements for the christening. On 28 July there was a more immediate cause for family celebration as Jackie celebrated her 34th birthday.

Above: 26 July 1963. the President broadcasts to the nation, describing the signing of the nuclear test ban treaty as "a victory for mankind". The agreement prohibited testing in the atmosphere, underwater and in space. Underground testing was excluded from the deal, but Kennedy still regarded this first major step along the disarmament road as one of his greatest achievements.

Opposite below: Jack and his sister-in-law, Lee Radziwill, looking solemn as they visit Jackie in hospital at Otis Air Force Base. Jackie had been rushed to hospital on 7 August, complaining of abdominal pain. An emergency Cesarean was performed and a 4lbs 10oz boy was born, five weeks premature. Jack had immediately flown from Andrews Air Base when he heard the news, but his son was born before he arrived at the hospital. Patrick Bouvier Kennedy suffered from hyaline membrane disease, the same respiratory problem that had afflicted John Jr. He died on 9 August.

United in grief

Opposite: The President and his son received the unwarranted attention of photographers as they visited Jackie, two days after Patrick's death. It was John Jr's first visit since his mother was taken into hospital. He was too young to take in what had happened; Caroline, on the other hand, was looking forward to having a baby brother or sister, and was deeply upset when her father broke the news.

Above: Jack and Jackie leave Otis Hospital on 14 August, five days after Patrick's death. Many commentators noted the fact that they left for Squaw Island hand in hand, as Jackie usually trailed behind her husband when they were walking together in public. The unity that this change suggested was genuine: the loss of their third child had a profound effect on their relationship.

Above: A tired Caroline cuddles up to her father aboard the yacht *Marlin*, summer 1963. A few days before Jackie was rushed into hospital, Jack had surprised the family by bringing home some puppies. His attempt to divert the children, who were becoming restless waiting for the new arrival, helped in the weeks following Patrick's death. Jack needed no such distraction. He made regular shuttle trips between Washington and Cape Cod to see Jackie. He appeared to take the loss even harder than his wife, as he had guilt and remorse to contend with, as well as grief.

Left: Jack accompanies John Jr, Caroline and their cousins to the candy store at Hyannis Port.

Opposite: John Jr plays at being skipper, late August 1963. He was intelligent and talkative, endlessly fascinated by the world around him, particularly all things mechanical.

Left: The Attorney General testifies before a Senate committee on organized crime. RFK's war on the Mafia was certainly not the accommodation the mobsters expected after their "contribution" to the 1960 election victory. When the President's connection with Judith Campbell - and thus Sam Giancana - was revealed in 1975, many believed it strengthened the case that the Mafia was behind the events in Dallas. This was further fueled when Giancana himself was murdered the same year.

Jackie heads for Europe

Opposite: 1 October 1963. The President and First Lady greet Emperor Haile Selassie of Ethiopia at Union Station, Washington. The 73-year-old Lion of Judah was yet another world leader who fell under Jackie's spell, despite the fact that the First Lady was at a low ebb and desperate to leave for Europe. Her sister Lee had invited her to join a party on board Aristotle Onassis's yacht *Christina*. Lee's affair with the buccaneering tycoon was providing the gossip columnists with a rich source of material.

Above: Receiving Emperor Haile Selassie was Jackie's first official engagement since Patrick's death seven weeks earlier. She left for Greece during the state banquet given in honor of the Ethiopian leader's visit. Jack had had reservations about the trip. It had already attracted a lot of adverse publicity, something which had always been an important benchmark for him. On this occasion his concern for Jackie's welfare overrode public relations considerations.

Public anger over late-night revelling

Left: Jackie on vacation in Greece, October 1963. The wave of public sympathy for the First Lady after the loss of her baby turned to anger when details of her trip were published. Stanislaus Radziwill, along with Franklin Delano Roosevelt Jr and his wife, had joined the party at Jack's behest, but it failed to have the desired effect. The public saw through the veneer of respectability this was meant to give, and stories of late-night revelling did not go down well.

Below: In addition to the bad publicity surrounding the First Lady's European trip, the President had many weighty political matters to occupy him in early October. He met with Britain's Foreign Secretary Lord Home as the situation in South Vietnam was reaching a crisis point. A matter of days later, Jack's close political ally Harold Macmillan resigned from office, and Sir Alec Douglas Home replaced him as Britain's prime minister.

Opposite: 7 October 1963. The President signs the nuclear test ban treaty, an historic first step on the road to ending the arms race. Kennedy described it as "a message of hope for all the world".

Opposite: Jack regularly took to his rocking chair to help relieve his back pain. He is pictured just after UN Ambassador Adlai Stevenson had returned from a trip to Dallas, where he received an extremely hostile reception. Placards of the President bearing the legend "Wanted For Treason" had been brandished, an indication that many of the citizens there regarded the recent test ban treaty as a sell-out. These events are said to have left the president in a fatalistic mood as his own trip to Texas approached.

Left: Jack at a Harvard-Columbia football game with Senator Ed Muskie, 19 October 1963. Jackie had returned from Europe two days earlier. There were rumors about impropriety during the trip, but the tender love letters Jackie wrote while she was away suggest otherwise. The First Lady seemed reinvigorated when she returned, and soon decided she wanted to play an active role in Jack's re-election campaign. She agreed to accompany her husband on his forthcoming visit to Texas, her first domestic political trip as First Lady.

Below: Rose Kennedy gives a forthright television interview on the subject of handicapped children. The family had long dissembled on the subject of Rosemary, who had in fact been at St Coletta's School, Jefferson, Wisconsin since 1949. After Joe's death in 1969, Rose regularly visited her eldest daughter.

Misunderstanding on South Vietnam

1 November 1963. Events in Saigon go to the top of the political agenda as Jack is awakened with the news that a coup has unseated South Vietnam's leader Ngo Dinh Diem. The United States had an ambivalent attitude toward the Diem regime. As a putatively pro-Western, anti-Communist state, it had enjoyed American support. However, persecution of the country's Buddhists had led to many horrifying acts of self-immolation. In late August, the President, distracted by grief, gave tacit approval for a military coup. He did so believing his top advisers thought this was the best course of action. They, in turn, consented, thinking they were carrying out the President's orders. By the time the misunderstanding came to light, events in South Vietnam took on a momentum of their own, culminating in the overthrow of Diem on 1 November. Diem and his brother, Ngo Dinh Nhu, were murdered, filling Jack with a deep sense of personal responsibility.

The President and First Lady pictured on the White House lawn, where they witnessed a parade by the Black Watch Royal Highland Regiment. Jackie had had second thoughts about the trip to Texas, which was now just a week away, but seeing how badly affected Jack was by recent events in South Vietnam, she resolved to put aside her concerns and accompany her husband.

Jack's moral dimension

Below: The bond between Jack and Jackie was stronger than ever in the fall of 1963. With Jackie intent on playing an active campaigning role in 1964, the future looked bright. Jack's popularity rating with the voters was higher than ever, and with the First Lady adding her singular appeal, it presented a formidable obstacle for the likely Republican candidate, Barry Goldwater. The first hurdle was the Texas trip, however, and Jack was keen to get that out of the way, particularly the visit to Dallas, widely regarded as the most anti-Democratic city in the country.

Opposite: Jack in pensive mood, two days before the Texas trip. He had just paid what was to be his last visit to his father. In the two years since Joe's debilitating stroke, Jack's decision-making had become increasingly informed by a new moral dimension. Joe's mantra, to do whatever it took to succeed, had got Jack to the White House. It was no longer his way, either in his public or personal life. Harold Macmillan undoubtedly played a key role in bringing out Jack's core decency, a determination to do the right thing, even if it went against self-interest.

Left: Jack smiles as John Jr skips after attending a ceremony at Arlington National Cemetery in November 1963.

CHAPTER SEVEN
Dallas:
22 November 1963

There was a sense of foreboding in the Kennedy camp about the trip to Dallas. UN Ambassador Adlai Stevenson had visited the city the previous month and been given a hostile reception. Even Lyndon Johnson, one of the state's own sons, had fallen from favor, and there were no guarantees that his presence on the ticket for 1964 would reap electoral rewards. Texas was an important part of the re-election campaign, and to visit the state and not go to Dallas was unthinkable.

The whistle-stop tour was to take in five venues over two days. On the morning of 22 November, the Kennedys left Fort Worth for Dallas, the fourth leg of the trip. Things had gone well so far, the President and First Lady having been warmly received in San Antonio and Houston. There had been concerns that Jackie might be given a torrid time following a recent solo trip to Greece. She had received a lot of bad press over alleged revelry aboard Aristotle Onassis's yacht. According to reports, such behavior ill became a woman who had so recently lost a child and whose husband was faced with such weighty affairs of state. These fears were quickly dispelled, however. Jackie carefully chose some conservative outfits for the Texas trip. This was a hedge against criticism that she was rather too fond of haute couture and life's luxuries, and lacked the common touch. Even so, she was the epitome of glamor and style and won the crowds over wherever she went. Halfway through the visit reports were already praising Jackie's sure-footed performance on the political stage and declaring her to be the jewel in the crown as far as her husband's re-election hopes were concerned.

The couple left Fort Worth for Dallas in buoyant mood. Thirteen minutes later, Air Force One touched down at Love Field and the President and First Lady were soon working a highly receptive crowd. At 11.55 they took their places on the raised rear seat of the Lincoln convertible. Governor Connally and his wife Nellie sat on the jump seats opposite. It was a bright, clear day and the vehicle's bulletproof bubble had been removed.

The motorcade made its way through the city, greeted enthusiastically by the crowds that lined the streets. The destination was the Trade Mart, where Jack was to make a speech. As the Lincoln turned into Dealey Plaza, three shots rang out. The first bullet struck Jack in the back. Before Secret Servicemen could reach the vehicle, the second bullet hit him in the back of the head. Governor Connally was also shot and seriously wounded. Jackie cradled her husband's head as the car sped to Parkland Hospital, just a few minutes' drive away. Kennedy's heart was still beating and the trauma team attempted a tracheotomy. But with virtually the entire right side of the brain now missing, it was a hopeless task. John F Kennedy was declared dead at 1.00 p.m.

The security men who first attended the President knew there was no hope. The injuries were so appalling that some instinctively ran to Lyndon Johnson's car, which was some way behind the President's in the motorcade. Ninety-eight minutes after Kennedy was pronounced dead, Johnson took the 40-word oath of office and was

Jackie is presented with a bouquet of red roses as cheering crowds greet the arrival of Air Force One at Love Field, Dallas, 22 November 1963. The previous day she had been given yellow roses, the traditional symbol of the Lone Star state. The flowers were placed on the back seat of the Lincoln, between her and her husband, for the motorcade journey into the city.

Above: A family grieves. Caroline Kennedy had been excited at the thought of sleeping over at a friend's house on the night of 22 November, the first time she had done so. The trip was hastily canceled and the children's nurse, Maud Shaw, broke the news to her. John Jr's age made it difficult for him to take in what had happened.

sworn in as the 36th President of the United States. The brief ceremony took place aboard Air Force One, which was taking both him and Kennedy's body back to Washington. Jackie stood beside Johnson as he took the oath, her clothes still spattered with her husband's blood and tissue.

Within a matter of hours the police had a suspect in custody. Lee Harvey Oswald, a 24-year-old former marine, had lived in the Soviet Union between 1959 and 1962. He worked as a clerk at the Texas School Book Depository on Elm Street, and police quickly concluded that this was the building from which the shots had been fired. A carbine and three empty shells were discovered on the 6th floor, and the weapon was traced back to Oswald. He was charged with murder, although rumors of a larger conspiracy began circulating almost immediately.

On 24 November, Oswald himself was shot and killed while being moved from the local police station to the state prison. In the two days he had spent in custody he had not confessed to firing the gun which killed Kennedy and wounded Connally. The man who shot him was Jack Ruby, a Dallas nightclub owner. Ruby was arrested and later convicted of Oswald's murder.

President Johnson set up a commission under Chief Justice Earl Warren to investigate the events of 22 November. The report was delivered 10 months later, on 27 September 1964, and concluded that Oswald had acted alone. Ruby had perpetrated an individual act of revenge. In short, there was no wider conspiracy. These findings did nothing to end speculation. Between them Jack and Bobby had peered into some murky waters and made many enemies. They had taken on Jimmy Hoffa and the Teamsters Union; there had been dubious connections with the Mafia; Castro and the Kremlin also came under suspicion, while some thought it more than coincidental that the assassination followed so closely on the heels of Diem's murder in South Vietnam. Bobby was among the first to wonder if the CIA were implicated.

Rumors persisted for 15 years, when the House Select Committee on Assassinations finally shed new light on what happened in Dallas. Acoustics experts revealed that shots were fired from the grassy knoll on Dealey Plaza, as well as from the book depository. The identity of the perpetrators was - and remains - a mystery, but at least the theory of a disaffected individual was finally disproved.

John F. Kennedy took office determined to make his mark on history. Lyndon Johnson accepted the vice-presidency wondering whether yet another first executive would die in office and propel him into the top job. The events of Dallas, 22 November 1963 turned conjecture into reality for both men.

For a long time accounts of Kennedy's life and work became more akin to hagiography. His premature and violent death meant that his good qualities and achievements were magnified, his shortcomings and failures overlooked. The fact is that until November 1960 he knew more about how to win power than what to do with it. After taking office, he found that the learning curve was steep, and there were many reverses along the way. He grew in stature during his 1000-day tenure of the White House, and by the time of his death he was on the threshold of greatness.

But the balance-sheet approach fails to take account of the emotional impact Kennedy had, both on the American people and those beyond its shores. The world he envisioned, the ideals he espoused, described as they were so memorably, touched people's lives in a way few statesmen have managed to do, either before or since. He was more than an inspiring politician; he symbolized the hopes and dreams of a generation.

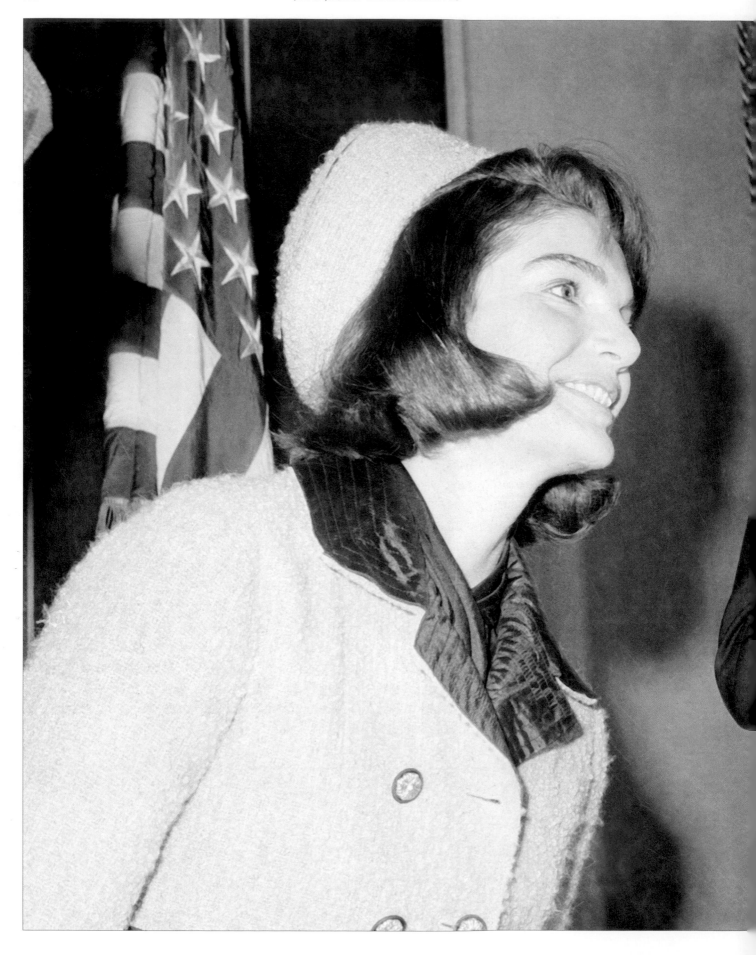

The President joins in the applause for the First Lady at a Chamber of Commerce breakfast, Fort Worth, on the morning of Friday, 22 November 1963. The Kennedys had arrived at 11:00 p.m. the previous evening, having earlier visited San Antonio and Houston. Jack had already made one impromptu speech that morning, going down to the hotel parking lot to greet the assembled well-wishers. The crowd wanted Jackie, to which the President responded: "Mrs Kennedy is organizing herself. It takes a little longer but, of course, she looks better than we do when she does it". The President's visit was not met with universal good humor. *The Dallas Morning News* had a lot of barbed comment, including a full-page advertisement welcoming the president - surrounded by a black border. When Jack saw the hostile press reports, he declared that he and Jackie were in "nut country".

The final journey

Opposite above: Jackie sits between the President and Governor John Connally as the motorcade journey gets underway. As they made their way into Dallas, Connally took his place in the jump seat opposite, next to his wife. Jack told Jackie to concentrate her attention on the crowd lining the street to her left, while he acknowledged those on his side; it was unnecessary duplication for both to woo the same voter. Jackie wanted to wear sunglasses to shield her eyes from the blinding sun. Ever the politician, Jack realized the importance of eye contact and asked her to remove them. These were the last words he spoke to her.

Opposite below: The glorious weather meant that the presidential Lincoln had had its bulletproof bubble removed. Behind came four police motorcyclists and a limousine carrying several Secret Service personnel. On the running boards were agents Hill and Ready, who were charged with the protection of the President and First Lady respectively.

Above: Jackie cradles her husband as he slumps in his seat. The first bullet struck the President in the back of the neck, exited the throat and hit Governor Connally. The second shattered Kennedy's skull. He was still alive on arrival at Parkland Memorial Hospital but there was no hope that he could have survived such terrible injuries.

"I want them to see what they have done"

Above: Lyndon and Lady Bird Johnson comfort Jackie aboard Air Force One. The relationship between the Johnsons and the Kennedys was cool at best, but Jackie had always got on well with the vice-president. She refused to change out of her blood-spattered pink woolen suit, declaring "I want them to see what they have done".

Opposite below: Jackie accompanies her husband's body to Bethesda Naval Hospital, where the mandatary autopsy was to be performed. It was there that Bobby met her. He had been at his Hickory Hill home when news of his brother's death came through. He had spent the morning in meetings to do with the ongoing war on organized crime. When the lone gunman theory was eventually discredited, there was much speculation regarding Mafia involvement.

Opposite above: RFK and some of his children, pictured shortly after he was informed of his brother's death. Bobby was the mainstay of the family in the aftermath of the tragedy. He was both practical and a source of great emotional support to others, though inconsolable himself.

Johnson: the 36th President

Jackie witnesses the swearing in of Lyndon Baines Johnson as 36th President of the United States. The brief ceremony took place aboard Air Force One, which then left for Washington. JFK's body was in the rear of the plane. Hurried phone calls had been made to ascertain who had the authority to administer the 40-word oath. Bobby Kennedy himself was consulted in his role as Attorney General. He confirmed that US District Judge Sarah Hughes could perform the ceremony. Johnson officially took office 98 minutes after JFK was pronounced dead.

"He belongs to the country"

Above: Sunday 24 November. Members of the Kennedy family stand together at the Capitol Rotunda to listen to a eulogy for the late President. By the next morning, a quarter of a million people had filed past the casket. The protocol for lying-in-state was for the casket to remain open, but Jackie felt her husband's body, drained of blood, looked like a waxwork figure and refused. She also stood firm on the choice of burial place. The Kennedy clan favored the family plot at Brookline. It was Jackie who insisted on the national cemetery at Arlington, commenting: "He belongs to the country".

Opposite: Jackie holds the flag which was draped over her husband's coffin. She won universal admiration for the stoicism and dignity with which he bore her loss. Many described her deportment and demeanor on the day of the funeral as regal.

Following pages: At his mother's prompting, John Jr executed a faultless salute after the service at St Matthew's Cathedral. Previously he had never quite managed to get it right. The day of the funeral was John Junior's third birthday. Caroline was six two days later, 27 November 1963. Breaking with tradition, Jackie insisted on walking behind the gun carriage which bore the casket. A riderless black horse followed, with a sheathed sword and boots reversed in the stirrups, indicating that a commander-in-chief had fallen. President de Gaulle, Haile Selassie and Prince Philip, Duke of Edinburgh were among the dignitaries in attendance. One notable absentee was Jack's mentor and friend, Harold Macmillan, who was too ill to travel.

Left: This photograph was a key exhibit in the Warren Commission's investigation into the events of 22 November 1963. It shows Oswald holding the same Mannlicher-Carcano rifle that was found on the sixth floor of the Texas School Book Depository. The ten-month inquiry produced a 10 million-word report with a simple conclusion: that both Oswald and Ruby had acted alone. It was later alleged that the photograph of Oswald was a fake, and in 1978 acoustics experts revealed that there had been a second gunman. The following year, the doubts raised led the House Assassinations Committee to conclude that the President had been the victim of a wider conspiracy, although the identity of the perpetrators remained a mystery.

Below: On the day of JFK's funeral, Jack Ruby is transferred from Dallas city jail (gaol?) to the county facility. Twenty-four hours earlier Ruby had shot Lee Harvey Oswald, the man accused of assassinating the President, when he was being escorted on the same journey.

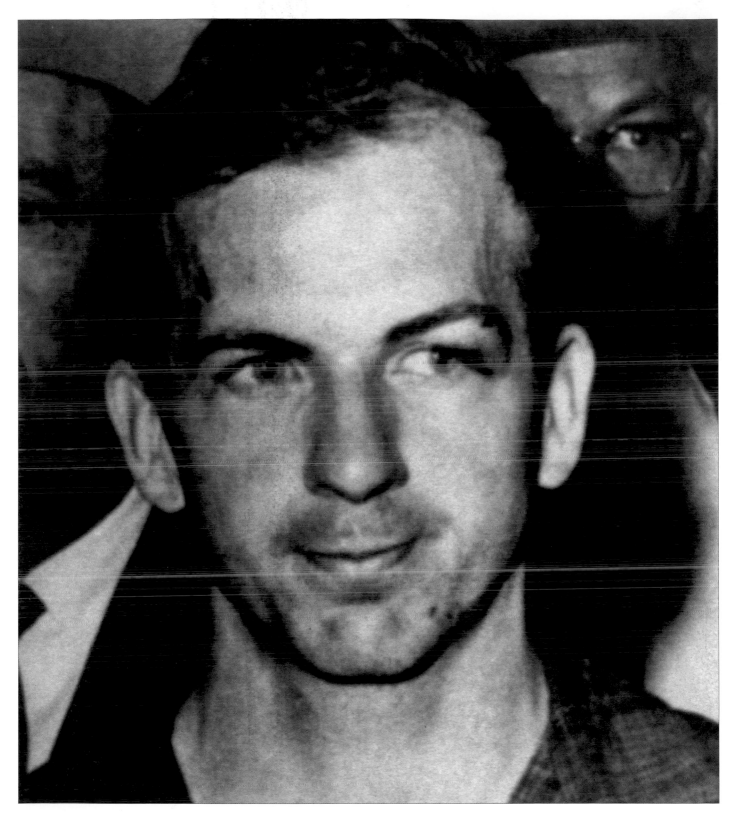

Lee Harvey Oswald charged 。

Above: Within hours of Kennedy's assassination, Lee Harvey Oswald was arrested and charged with murder. A 24-year-old disaffected former marine, Oswald worked at the Texas School Book Depository, the building which had housed the assassin, according to Dallas Police. Oswald himself was shot by nightclub owner Jack Ruby on Sunday 24 November while he was being transferred to the county jail. He died 48 hours later at Parkland Memorial Hospital, having been attended by some of the same doctors who had fought to save the President. In the two days he spent in custody he did not confess to Kennedy's murder.

CHAPTER EIGHT
Jackie
1963-1994

If the Kennedys were America's royalty, Jackie was undoubtedly the queen. The manner in which she endured her husband's death had a majestic quality and endeared her to the public even more.

After the pomp and ceremony of the funeral, the following months brought home the full impact of bereavement. Naturally, the toll was primarily emotional. Jackie lapsed into a deep depression, often weeping uncontrollably. Away from her children's gaze she sought to alleviate her pain with vodka and chain-smoking. But there were practical considerations to be dealt with. She was a thiry-four-year-old widow who had to plan a secure future for herself and her children. Decisions had to be made, not all of them within her control. There was the immediate question of a family home. Jackie left the White House for the last time on 6 December 1963. Averell Harriman gave her the temporary use of his Georgetown house, and in early 1964 Jackie bought a property of her own nearby. She was a regular visitor at Arlington. Just as she had insisted on an eternal flame at Jack's grave, so it became important to her to honor his name and glorify his achievements. The days of Camelot were over, but she could preserve its spirit, its noble aims and heroic deeds. It was a myth, of course, and over time the veneer would become tarnished.

The way in which Jackie held true to the romanticized view of the White House days even extended to the speculation about who was behind the events of 22 November 1963. She could not bear the thought that Lee Harvey Oswald, "a silly little Communist", had brought the days of poetry and power to an end. The theory that right-wing extremists had been responsible was more palatable, for it made Jack a martyr to his liberal values. If the days of Camelot were over, then that ultimate sacrifice was a fitting end. Her memory of Jack as a husband took on a similar hue. She cleaved to the best of their ten-year marriage, and clung to the belief that despite all the infidelity she held a unique place in his heart.

Jackie was inundated with requests to attend memorial services and dedication ceremonies. She refused most, but there were some which had a particular resonance. One of those was at Runnymede, England, where a monument was built on land ceded to the United States in perpetuity. It was a site of key importance in the history of the British constitution, and as such Jackie knew it would have struck a chord with Jack. Moreover, the address was given by Harold Macmillan, a friend to both and mentor to the former President.

By the middle of 1964, Jackie realized that she could not remain in Washington. Much as she needed to preserve the Camelot idyll, she found she couldn't do it so close to the seat of power. Her Georgetown home had become almost a tourist attraction, taking away all hope of privacy for herself and a relatively normal upbringing for her children.

At the very time when Jackie resolved to move to New York, she found that Bobby had decided to do the same. He left the Johnson administration to run for the Senate. He couldn't remain in a government he regarded as tainted, led by a man he saw as a usurper. Despite his fine laudatory words in public, Johnson was the last man to pick up the baton and run with the precepts of the New Frontier.

Bobby had been Jackie's chief source of comfort. The two were virtually inseparable in the spring and summer of 1964, to such an extent that rumors of a more intimate relationship began to circulate. Close as they

Above: 14 January 1964. Jackie makes her first public statement since the assassination. She had received 800,000 letters of condolence.

were, in the aftermath of the assassination Jackie and Bobby were at odds over LBJ. To Jackie he was warm and sympathetic. He even offered her an ambassadorship, but after flirting with the idea Jackie turned it down. Bobby made good use of their relationship when he turned his attention to establishing fitting memorials to his brother's name. It was he who suggested that Cape Canaveral and Idlewild Airport be renamed in Jack's honor, using Jackie as the conduit to the man in whose gift such decisions lay.

While Bobby was running for senator, Jackie fell

back on her usual occupations: riding, shopping, decorating and travel. In those early days she was a grieving widow and mother. It was only a matter of time before she, and others, saw her as a beautiful and available woman. There was an emotional void to fill, and Jackie embarked on a number of affairs. These included a relationship with Jack Warnecke, the architect who worked on the Arlington grave monument, and David Ormsby-Gore, Britain's ambassador to Washington, with whom both she and Jack had been good friends. When

Ormsby-Gore's wife Sissie died in 1967, they were free to marry. But Jackie would choose someone more exotic, more dangerous - and immeasurably richer - when she next contemplated a marriage partner.

Jackie's life became more settled, more purposeful, and in March 1968 she was positively rejuvenated when Bobby decided to run for President. Early apprehensions were replaced by a sense of euphoria as the prospect of a new Camelot emerged. "Won't it be wonderful when we get back in the White House?" she beamed on one occasion. It was a short-lived dream. On 5 June 1968, having just secured victory in the California primary, Bobby was shot by Sirhan Sirhan in the Ambassador Hotel, Los Angeles. It came a matter of weeks after Martin Luther King's assassination, and Jackie was deeply traumatized. These were violent times to be living in America, and soon the ideal escape route presented itself.

Aristotle Onassis was a buccaneering tycoon, his empire including Olympic Airways. There were shades of "Black Jack" Bouvier in him, and though he didn't have Jack's looks, he was extremely attractive to women. However, the main attraction for Jackie was undoubtedly the fact that Onassis's vast resources offered her and the children total protection. For Onassis's part, he was a notorious pursuer and collector of beautiful women. His affair with diva Maria Callas had ended his marriage, and when he first met Jackie six years earlier, he was her sister's lover. Jackie was a prize trophy, in a league of her own. The two were married on the island of Skorpios, 20 October 1968.

Below: Caroline, Jackie and John Jr during a family vacation in Irelend, June 1967.

The Kennedy family preferred her in the role of Jack's widow. It was one thing to contemplate the idea of Jackie remarrying, quite another for her choose someone like Onassis: not only coarse but persona non grata to the US authorities. Bobby had been concerned that the relationship might have damaged his election chances, but that was academic now. The American public were equally dismayed, seeing it as a betrayal of Jack's memory. As Onassis was a divorcé, even the Vatican presented a problem. Ironically, one person who did give the union her blessing was Rose Kennedy. She had met Onassis and found him quite charming. As a rough-edged entrepreneur seeking to marry a socialite, perhaps Rose found echoes of her own courtship. She and Jackie were warmer to each other now than they had ever been when Jack was alive.

The marriage began well, as both got exactly what they wanted from the relationship. She launched into refurbishing their island home, while he continued to pay regular visits to La Callas; there was already an element of déja-vu. She had even less to do with Onassis's business dealings than she had with Jack's political life.

The marriage ended on 15 March 1975 with Onassis's death. Effectively, however, it had been over a long time before then. Onassis was practical, acquisitive and easily bored. Jackie was ageing. Her long absences in the United States rankled; being a free spirit was not part of the lot of a Greek wife. And despite his enormous wealth, he also took umbrage at her lavish spending, yet another echo of the past. Superstition also played a part. The Onassis family was struck by a series of family tragedies, including the death of Ari's beloved son Alexander. The tycoon began to have business problems, including the loss of Olympic Airways in January 1975. Some laid the ill fortune at Jackie's door. Whether or not Onassis believed she was cursed, he wanted out.

He had to prepare the ground carefully before he could file for divorce. Under Greek law Jackie was entitled to one-eighth of his fortune, and he was keen to find ways to circumvent what he perceived as an over-generous settlement. In the event he succumbed to myasthenia gravis and the settlement became the subject of a protracted lawsuit.

Jackie began her new life back in New York, keeping Onassis's name and $26 million of his fortune - far more than he had wanted to bestow on her. The return to the United States coincided with some of the first revelations of Camelot's less seemly side. Jack's affairs with Judith Campbell and Mary Meyer became public, as did the singular ministrations of Dr Feel Good.

Jackie took up residence at 1040 Fifth Avenue, and also acquired a private realm: 400 acres on Martha's Vineyard, on which she built a house overlooking the ocean. She also got a job. Jackie joined the publishing house Viking, working as a part-time book editor. It was her first paid employment since her brief flirtation with photojournalism some 25 years earlier. She couldn't escape her celebrity, of course, and there was always the suggestion that people were interested in her for who she was rather than what she could do. From the public perspective, she was also criticized for being an immensely wealthy widow "playing" at being a modern single working woman. In fact, she cared passionately about the projects she worked on, but at Viking she couldn't win. She took up a similar job at Doubleday in 1978, and there things went much better. Her colleagues protected her from unwanted attention, but also accepted her as a member of the team. She remained there until her death.

Jackie's later years brought contentment away from work too, including further romance. The new man in her life was Maurice Tempelsman, a diamond merchant whom she had known since her days as First Lady. He took over the running of her financial affairs and they became close. He lacked the scintillating presence, raw appeal and dangerous edge of her first two husbands. But as Jackie turned fifty in 1979, his qualities of dependability and gentleness more than compensated. The two were able to converse in French and shared a love of the arts. Tempelsman was married and for a long time their affair remained clandestine. He and his wife separated in 1982, and Tempelsman eventually moved into Jackie's Fifth Avenue apartment. They didn't marry.

Tempelsman's devotion to Jackie extended to her children. By now, however, Jackie was keen to see Caroline and John making their own way in the world, free of any family encumbrances. In 1980 Caroline graduated from Radcliffe College, Harvard with a degree in fine arts. She got a job in the media department of the Metropolitan Museum of Art. Caroline shared Jackie's love of horses and photography. She didn't have her mother's exotic beauty; that would skip a generation and manifest itself in her own children. In 1986 Caroline married Edwin

Above: Jackie and Onassis in London, September 1970. The death of Onassis's former sister-in-law in May of that year began a spate of family tragedies.

Schlossberg, whom she met while working at the Museum. Schlossberg was intelligent and cultured - and thirteen years her senior, almost exactly the age difference there had been between her parents. Jackie became a grandmother in 1988, when Caroline gave birth to a daughter, Rose. Tatiana arrived soon afterwards, and in January 1993 Caroline gave birth to John, who inevitably would be known as Jack.

John Jr. graduated from Brown University, Providence, Rhode Island, where he majored in American history. He went on to law school but later moved into journalism. He was tall, athletic and handsome, with the spark and wit of his father. Jackie was fiercely proud of both her children.

In late 1993 a lump was discovered in Jackie's groin and she was diagnosed as suffering from non-Hodgkin's lymphoma. She began a grueling course of chemotherapy, but when the cancer spread inexorably she asked for it to be stopped. She took the news stoically, comforted by the fact that she had helped her children recover from their tragic early loss and guided them into adulthood. She died 19 May 1994 and was buried alongside Jack at Arlington cemetery.

Jackie Kennedy Onassis rose to prominence through her first marriage, and maintained her profile through her second. Her achievements were modest, but to a generation she was the epitome of glamor and style. She was not the only woman whose look was envied and copied. However, Jackie fascinated as well as inspired. Despite her French ancestry and jet-set lifestyle, it was America where she held court. There were periods when the public's love for their adopted queen cooled. The affair endured, however; of that there can be no doubt.

14 May 1965, Runnymede, England. Seven-year-old Caroline Kennedy is overwrought at a memorial service for her father. Jackie declined many of the invitations to attend such ceremonies, but this had particular significance. Queen Elizabeth II dedicated a stone monument to her husband at the place where the signing of Magna Carta took place in 1215, a landmark in British constitutional history. She knew that would have meant a lot to Jack, as would the fact that his great friend and mentor Harold Macmillan gave an address.

Public hostility as Jackie weds Onassis

Opposite below: 20 October 1968. Jackie marries Aristotle Onassis on his private island, Skorpios. Onassis had proposed the previous spring, when Bobby Kennedy was a front-runner in the Presidential election. The Kennedys were unhappy about her choice of suitor and Jackie agreed to defer the wedding until after the election. Bobby's death changed all that and made her more determined than ever to leave the country.

Above: 24 June 1969. Jackie and Ari take refreshment on the Isle of Capri during a Mediterranean cruise. The first year of their marriage was a happy one, as both got exactly what they wanted from the relationship. Public reaction was hostile, however. Jackie was vilified for what was seen as selling herself to an uncouth tycoon.

Opposite above: 9 June 1968. Jackie, with her sister and children at Bobby Kennedy's grave, Arlington National Cemetery, Virginia. Jackie had been reinvigorated at the prospect of Bobby becoming President. His death caused her to retrench in fear and hastened her decision to exchange a violent America for marriage to Onassis and the security of Skorpios.

JFK Library finally completed

Above: Jackie arrives at Aktion Airport, Greece, having accompanied her husband's body from Paris, where he died on 15 March 1975. Jackie had been in New York at the time, the marriage having ended in all but name a long time before. There followed a bitter legal wrangle between Jackie and Onassis's daughter, Christina, over a financial settlement.

Opposite: 1 October 1979, Boston, Massachusetts. Jackie and John Jr at the dedication ceremony for the John Fitzgerald Kennedy Library. As this was a project that Jack himself had initiated, its completion had a special resonance for the family. Both Caroline and John Jr spoke at the ceremony, the latter reciting Stephen Spender's poem "I Think Continually Of Those Who Were Truly Great". Jackie was fiercely proud of both her children as they entered adulthood. She was especially pleased at the way they were able to honor their father's name without allowing the past to overshadow their lives.

Opposite above: Jackie discusses family matters with Teddy Kennedy shortly before he launched his campaign to win the Democratic nomination for President in 1979.

Opposite below: 5 June 1980. Caroline is congratulated by members of her family after graduating from Radcliffe College, Harvard. Caroline's looks were more Kennedy than Bouvier, but she shared her mother's passion for horses and photography. In 1981 she met Edwin Schlossberg, whom she married five years later.

Above: Jackie's serene beauty shows through in this picture. Her final years brought contentment, both in her professional and private life. She was a successful book editor, and enjoyed a close relationship with diamond merchant Morris Tempelsman.

Picture Credits

All photographs in this book are reproduced by kind permission of Corbis.

Bettmann / Corbis

1, 2, 3, 4, 7,8, 9 10/1114, 23,
25T, 29, 30, 31, 32, 33T, 34, 35,
36, 38, 39, 40, 41, 42, 43T, 43B,
44, 45T, 46, 47, 48, 49, 50, 51T,
51B, 52T, 56, 57T, 57B, 63, 66,
68, 69, 70, 78T, 78B, 79, 80, 81T,
81B, 82, 83, 84, 85T, 85B, 87,
90T, 90B, 91, 93, 95, 96, 98, 99T,
99B, 100, 102, 104, 105, 106,
107, 108T, 108B, 110, 113T,
113B, 114T, 114B, 115, 123,
126T, 126B, 124, 125, 132, 134,
135, 137, 138T, 139, 140, 141,
142T, 142B, 143T, 143B, 144,
145, 146, 147T, 148T, 148B,
149, 150, 151T, 151B, 152B,
153, 155T, 155B, 156, 158T,
158B, 159, 160, 161T, 161B,
162, 163, 164T, 164B, 165, 166,
167T, 167B, 168, 169T,
169B,170B, 172B, 173, 174, 175,
176T, 176B, 177, 178T, 178B,
179T, 179B, 180, 181T, 181B,
183, 184, 186T, 196B, 187, 188,
189, 192, 194, 196, 198, 199,
200T, 200B, 201, 202, 203, 204,
205, 206, 207T, 207B, 208,
209T, 209B, 210, 211T, 211B,
212, 213T, 213B, 214, 216, 217,
218, 220, 221T, 221B, 222T,
222B, 226, 227T, 227B, 228,
231T, 231B, 230, 232, 233T,
234T, 234B, 236, 237, 240T,

240B, 241, 242T, 242B, 243,
244, 245, 246, 248, 251, 252,
253, 254, 256, 257B, 258, 259T,
260, 262T, 262B, 263, 264, 267,
268, 269, 270, 271, 272, 274,
276, 277T, 277B, 278T, 278B,
279, 280, 281,282T, 282B, 283,
286, 288, 289, 290, 291B, 292,
295, 297, 298, 301, 302, 303,
304T, 304B, 305, 306, 307T,
309, 310, 312, 313T, 313B, 314,
316, 317T, 320T, 320B, 322T,
322B, 323, 324, 325T, 325B,
326, 328, 330T, 330B, 331, 332,
333, 336T, 336B, 337, 338T,
338B, 339, 340, 341T, 341B,342,
343, 344T, 344B,345, 346, 348,
352, 354T, 356T, 359, 360, 361,
362, 364B, 366, 368, 370, 371,
374, 376T, 376B, 377, 378,
380T, 380B, 382

Corbis

12, 16, 17, 20, 22, 25B, 26T,
26B, 28, 33B, 37T, 37B, 45B,
52B, 54T, 54B, 58T, 58B, 59, 60,
62, 71, 72, 76, 77, 86, 88, 89, 92,
120, 121, 127, 128, 129, 147B,
170T, 172T, 195, 224, 225,
233B, 238, 239, 275, 284, 287T,
291T, 293, 294, 307B, 308,
317B, 318, 319, 321, 334T,
334B, 335, 350, 354B, 355,357,
364T, 365

Hulton Deutsch/ Corbis

18, 235,373

**Underwood and Underwood/
Corbis:**

24, 118,

JFK Library/ Corbis Sygma

64/65

**Dan McElleney/ Bettmann
Corbis:**

109

**Herb Scharfman/ Bettmann
Corbis:**

111

Robert Levin/ Corbis Sygma:

138B

Randy Faris/ Corbis:

112

Ted Streshinsky/ Corbis:

259B

Wally McNamee/ Corbis:

356B, 379,

Robert Maass/ Corbis:

381

Every effort has been made to ensure that the copyright details shown are correct,
but if there are any inccauracies, please contact the publisher.

Bibliography

JFK Reckless Youth
Nigel Hamilton
Pimlico, London 2000

The Kennedys
Peter Collier & David Horowitz
Secker & Warburg, London 1984

J.F.K. A Hidden Life
Robin Cross
Bloomsbury 1992

One Thousand Days; John F. Kennedy in the White House
Arthur M. Schlesinger
Mariner Books, New York

The Kennedy Clan
John H. Davis
Sidgwick and Jackson, London 1985

To The Best Of My Ability
Ed. James M McPherson
Dorling Kindersley, London 2000

Mrs Kennedy
Barbara Leaming
Weidenfeld & Nicholson, London 2001

America's Queen
Sarah Bradford
Penguin, London 2000